# Counselling in
# Child Disability

*To Marcia, for producing a treasured son and grandson*

# Counselling in Child Disability

## Skills for working with parents

*Garry Hornby*
*BSc, MA, DipEdPsych, PhD*

Lecturer in Special Education,
Counselling and Educational Psychology
University of Hull

**CHAPMAN & HALL**

London · Glasgow · Weinheim · New York · Tokyo · Melbourne · Madras

hed by Chapman & Hall, 2–6 Boundary Row, London SE1 8HN, UK

nan & Hall, 2–6 Boundary Row, London SE1 8HN, UK

Academic & Professional, Wester Cleddens Road,
briggs, Glasgow G64 2NZ, UK

nan & Hall GmbH, Pappelallee 3, 69469 Weinheim, Germany

Chapman & Hall Inc., One Penn Plaza, 41st Floor, New York NY
10119, USA

Chapman & Hall Japan, Thomson Publishing Japan, Hirakawacho Nemoto
Building, 6F, 1-7-11 Hirakawa-cho, Chiyoda-ku, Tokyo 102, Japan

Chapman & Hall Australia, Thomas Nelson Australia, 102 Dodds
Street, South Melbourne, Victoria 3205, Australia

Chapman & Hall India, R. Seshadri, 32 Second Main Road, CIT East,
Madras 600 035, India

Distributed in the USA and Canada by Singular Publishing Group Inc.,
4284 41st Street, San Diego, California 92105

First edition 1994

© 1994 Garry Hornby

Typeset in 10/12pt Palatino by Mews Photosetting, Beckenham, Kent
Printed in Great Britain by St Edmundsbury Press, Bury St Edmunds,
Suffolk

ISBN 0 412 55350 3     1 56593 308 7 (USA)

A catalogue record for this book is available from the British Library

Library of Congress Catalog Card Number: 93–74903

∞ Printed on permanent acid-free text paper, manufactured in
accordance with ANSI/NISO Z39.48–1992 and ANSI/NISO
Z39.48–1984 (Permanence of Paper).

# Contents

# Preface

This book is mainly aimed at helping professionals who wish to improve their working relationships with parents of children with disabilities. However, much of what is included is applicable to professionals working with the families of adults with disabilities.

The contents of the book are based on my experience of working with children with disabilities, their parents and the professionals who work with them over a twenty year period in England, New Zealand, North America and India. During this time I have become more and more convinced that it is not the practitioners' expertise in their own professional area which is the key to effective intervention with such children but their interpersonal skills, attitudes and knowledge relevant to working with parents.

Therefore, this book is aimed at helping professionals in the health, education and welfare services who work with people with disabilities to improve their effectiveness in working with parents.

The first chapter provides a rationale for the importance of working effectively with parents of children with disabilities. The essential functions which professionals fulfil with these parents are discussed and the skills, attitudes and knowledge which professionals need for this aspect of their work are outlined. In Chapter 2 the effects of disability on parents and other family members are described. The process of adaptation to disability is discussed along with consideration of various models for how families function when they include children with disabilities. The models proposed and issues discussed in this chapter are further elaborated in Chapter 3 which includes the personal stories of two parents: a mother of a 12-year-old girl with profound hearing impairment; and the father of a 5-year-old girl with Down's syndrome. In Chapter 4 a model for working with parents is proposed. The model includes consideration of parents' needs and their potential contributions to professional interventions with children with disabilities. The model highlights the interpersonal skills which professionals need to develop in order to work effectively with parents. These skills are discussed in the following five chapters.

In Chapter 5 the importance of listening and the development of passive and active listening skills are discussed. Chapter 6 presents a three-stage model of counselling and discusses the professional skills needed to use the model in working with parents. In Chapter 7 assertiveness is discussed and the assertion skills needed by professionals and parents, in order for them to communicate effectively, are elaborated. Chapter 8 includes a description of the professional skills needed for involvement in various types of group work with parents of children with disabilities. In Chapter 9 the skills required for empowering, enabling and acting as mentors for parents and less experienced colleagues are considered and a model for stress management is discussed.

The final chapter provides a summary of the interpersonal skills, attitudes and knowledge covered in the book and considers ways in which professionals can increase their competency in these areas.

Garry Hornby
*Hull, 1994*

# Acknowledgements

Many people have helped me develop the ideas contained in this book and I would like to thank them all. Ray Murray has been a tremendous influence and personal mentor over many years. Professors Milton Seligman, Nirbhay Singh and John Allan have also been extremely helpful with different aspects of my work. I have enjoyed working with, learned from and owe a debt of gratitude to many other people, especially Heather Alford, Dianne Anderson, Dr Saroj Arya, Professor Ann Clarke, Dr Cliff Cunningham, Linda Davies, Vivienne Dockray, Debbie Espiner, Dr Hans Everts, Marie Flavell, Mike and Maria Higgs, Chris Hilton-Jones, Georgia Jensen-Procter, Robin Jones, Hans Levin, Rob Linton, Michelle Mann, Leslie Max, Dr David Mitchell, Alwyn Morgan, Sue O'Shea, Ros Ostick, Liz Painter, Reeta Peshawaria, Shirley Pethick, John Taylor-Smith, Tony White, Steve Whitfield and Sally Windeatt.

I would like to thank Mrs Ellen Pilgrim, and Mr and Mrs O'Hara of the Coral Reef Club, for their hospitality during a frenetic period of writing in Barbados.

I would also like to thank Rosemary Morris, Catherine Walker and Alison Wellbrook for their encouragement, guidance and efficiency throughout the publication process.

Finally, I would like to thank the parents of children with disabilities with whom I have worked over the years, for teaching me what is important and what is not, and for inspiring me to consolidate my thoughts on the topic with this book.

# 1

# Importance of working with parents

## 1.1 INTRODUCTION

It is said that most expectant parents at some stage think of the possibility that their child may be born with a disability of some kind. That many parents do have such thoughts is confirmed by the fact that the second question most parents ask at the birth, after establishing the sex, is whether the child is 'all right'.

The expected birth of our first child coincided with the writing of this book, which I began after spending twenty years working with parents of children with disabilities. On a routine antenatal visit to our family doctor, my wife and I were stunned to be told that she had contracted rubella! This was despite having tested positive for rubella antibodies at the beginning of the pregnancy and, as far as we knew, being vaccinated against the virus during her childhood. Having worked with children who were deaf, blind and mentally handicapped I was well aware of the possible consequences of the rubella virus. Of course we went straight home and looked up all we could find on rubella. Our books confirmed what our doctor had said, that the risk of possible damage to the baby was much greater in the first trimester of the pregnancy than in the third, when my wife had contracted the virus. My wife is a teacher so it is likely that she caught rubella from one of her pupils. We were well aware that this could have occurred at any stage of the pregnancy. Hopefully, we were lucky that it didn't happen in the first three months! However, we still spent considerable time in the weeks leading up to the birth worrying about whether the baby would be affected, feeling guilty about having allowed this to happen, and thinking about how we would cope as parents of a child with a disability if the baby had been damaged by the rubella virus in some way.

To make matters worse two weeks before our child was due to be born I watched a television programme about a number of children born at a nearby hospital who had suffered brain damage during the birth process. Their parents were suing the hospital for negligence. I thought of all the children I had worked with over the years who had apparently been brain damaged during their birth and wondered how many of these could perhaps have been avoided. I also made careful note of the various indications of possible problems, such as the baby's heart rate dropping below 100 beats per minute, and was determined to watch these very carefully during the birth of our baby.

When my wife's waters broke we went into the hospital quite confidently in the knowledge that, apart from the rubella infection, the pregnancy had gone well and my wife was in excellent health. After several hours in the labour ward we were told that my wife's blood pressure had become too high and the baby was showing signs of distress. My wife was then attached to various drips and monitors which displayed her blood pressure, heart rate, contractions and the baby's heart rate. Needless to say I watched these monitors like a hawk! After a traumatic few hours our son was delivered with the aid of forceps by a doctor who had been on duty for most of the 22 hours we had been on the labour ward!

Immediately after the birth our son was given Apgar scores of nine by the paediatrician and eight by the midwife, so he appeared to have come through the birth process relatively unscathed. However, we were informed that, because of the rubella infection, a section of the umbilical cord was being sent to the laboratory for analysis, the results of which we would be given in due course. At four months of age an appointment was arranged for us with an audiologist who detected no abnormality in his hearing. At six months we saw a paediatrician who told us that the rubella virus had indeed passed through the cord to the baby. His examination found no abnormalities with the baby's heart, which we had not previously realized was another possible consequence of the rubella infection. The paediatrician told us that he would arrange for our son's vision to be tested and for us to return to the paediatric clinic at ten months and 18 months so that his development could be checked. At this stage, our son appears to be developing normally. However, our concerns about the effects of the rubella virus and the traumatic birth have served as a reminder of the potentially devastating impact of disability on parents, and of the necessity for professionals to be highly skilled in working with parents, as well as reinforcing the fact that anyone can become a parent of a child with a disability.

In fact, I had often asked myself why I had developed this interest in working with parents. I had observed that many of the people who worked in this field did so partly because they had experienced disability in their families, but this wasn't the case with me. Was this interest of mine some form of divine preparation for the time when I might become the parent of a child with a disability? Or perhaps, less eerily, was it related to my awareness of the serendipity of the incidence of disability, that it could happen to anyone, including me. Or was my interest in this field perhaps more to do with my feelings of inadequacy in dealing with the parents of children with disabilities early in my career, which had challenged me to find out more about how to work effectively with them?

I had certainly come across a wide range of parental reactions to disability in my work as a residential social worker, teacher, educational psychologist, researcher and lecturer in special education. I had seen some parents who were struggling to cope with seemingly impossible situations, and others where the child with the disability appeared to simply fit into family life and even contribute positively to it. This led to my fascination with understanding how such differences came about and more importantly, how professionals could help the parents who were experiencing difficulties.

When I was asked to write an article on this topic some years ago, while working in New Zealand, I decided to get some feedback on the draft version from various people including a parent of a child with Down's syndrome. The comments I received from this parent made a big impact on me. She pointed out that professionals seldom realize the tremendous power they have to support and help parents. Her own experiences and those of other parents she had talked to confirmed that professionals who work with children with disabilities are in a position in which they can be an important source of emotional and practical support but they can also be hurtful to parents. She considered that whether practitioners have a positive or negative influence on parents seems to depend more on their personalities than on their professional expertise. These comments, along with my own experiences in the field, have led me to believe that the competence of professionals in working with parents is as important as expertise in their own professional areas, in determining the effectiveness of their work with children with disabilities.

Most professionals who work with children or adults with disabilities would agree that involving parents in their interventions increases their effectiveness. They also realize that parents, and other family members, have their own needs which professionals must address if these families are to function well and provide optimum care for their disabled members. However, despite the obvious benefits of working with parents in these ways, training programmes for professionals who work with people with disabilities in the health, education and social welfare fields typically include little or nothing on the competencies necessary for effective parent involvement.

A possible source of help for parents are professionally trained counsellors. However, counsellor training courses generally pay little attention to working with people with disabilities and their families and few practising counsellors have expertise in this area (Lombana, 1989; Hornby and Seligman, 1991). Another problem, is that in many countries, such as Great Britain and India, the majority of parents are reluctant to seek professional counselling for any reason. In contrast to North America, where there are generally positive attitudes to seeking therapy, in Great Britain there appears to be a view that asking for help is a sign of weakness and that one must be virtually 'dangling from the light shade' before needing counselling! Therefore, parents of children with disabilities are typically reluctant to seek professional counselling. They are much more likely to bring their concerns to the professionals who work directly with their children, such as speech therapists, social workers, doctors, health visitors, teachers and psychologists. So it is left to practitioners in these disciplines, to do their best to develop their expertise in working with parents, since they are likely to be the main source of professional help for families who have members with disabilities (Dunst, Trivette and Deal, 1988).

Webster and Ward (1993) recently suggested that there are four major ways in which professionals can be of help to parents. First, they can help by effectively communicating to parents the specialist information they have. One of parents' greatest needs is for information about the disability itself and about the various services and agencies which are available to help them and their children. Second, professionals can help by carefully listening to the valuable information which parents have on their children. Parents often feel that they have much more which they need to tell professionals than they get the chance to communicate. Third, professionals can help parents to clarify their own feelings and thoughts about their children. Many parents need considerable help in order to come to terms with the disability. Professionals who work with their children are a possible source of this help. Fourth, professionals can offer parents alternative strategies for facilitating their children's development and changing their behaviour. Involving parents in a programme of activities with their children not only promotes the children's development but also helps to increase parents' confidence levels and thereby contributes to their adaptation to the situation they find themselves in. So to be more specific, what then are some essential functions professionals can fulfil for parents?

## 1.2 ESSENTIAL FUNCTIONS OF PROFESSIONALS

Four important functions of professionals who work with parents of children with disabilities are discussed below.

These are: communicating the diagnosis of disability, or the results of assessments, to parents, in a sensitive and constructive manner; providing information about the disability, services available, and on facilitating the child's development; providing emotional support, and helping parents to understand their feelings and reactions; and, linking parents with others who are in a similar position to themselves.

### 1.2.1 Communicating the results of diagnoses or assessments

The vast majority of people prefer to be told diagnostic or assessment results by a professional who communicates empathy, sensitivity, openness, and a positive yet realistic outlook. This person should be knowledgeable about the possible causes and likely consequences of the disability and of the services available. People prefer to be told as soon as possible after a diagnosis is made, or a problem becomes apparent, with both of them together and, if appropriate, with the disabled family member present. They want to be told in a private place with no disturbances, and to have adequate time for information to be given, questions asked, and further interviews scheduled (Cunningham, Morgan and McGucken, 1984).

When communication is handled in this way family members tend to adapt more quickly and establish more positive relationships with each other, the child with the disability, and professionals. However, many consultations with families are not conducted in this way, particularly initial diagnoses (Hornby, 1987). Many parents are angry and resentful about the way they were first told of the disability. One father with a multiply-handicapped son told me that the paediatrician who diagnosed the disability was, 'as subtle as an air raid'! This first, negative contact with a professional concerned with their child can sour parents' attitudes to future relationships with other professionals. It is therefore essential that all professionals follow the above guidelines when communicating such information to parents or other family members.

## 1.2.2 Providing information

One of the very first requests of parents, after receiving the diagnosis, is for comprehensive, accurate and up-to-date information about the child's disability (Philip and Duckworth, 1982). Most parents also want suggestions about what they can do to facilitate the child's development. Parents should also be told, at this time, about all the services and benefits available to help them care for their children. This information is widely available in the form of both written materials and professional knowledge (Hornby, 1991; Stone and Taylor, 1977). It is therefore quite alarming to discover how often it does not get to the people who need it. Professionals should therefore always check that parents have all the information they need about their child's disability and that they know about the relevant agencies and support groups which operate in their community. Making sure that parents know about the various grants and government benefits for which they are eligible is particularly important.

## 1.2.3 Providing support

Soon after the diagnosis parents and other family members need to have supportive counselling available to them. In many cases this is provided by members of the extended family, or friends or by other parents who have children with disabilities. But professionals also need to be able to provide this kind of support. Parents need someone to help them express and clarify their feelings and to help in understanding their reactions and those of others around them (Furneaux, 1988). In this way family members can be assisted to make a speedy and successful adaptation to the situation. If they do not receive such counselling they may experience considerable anguish and take much longer to move through the adaptation process (which is described in detail in Chapter 2). However, parents will seldom directly ask for counselling whereas they will ask for information or express concerns about their children. This then provides an opportunity for professionals to address these issues and to use their counselling skills to deal with any other concerns parents may have and thereby facilitate their movement through the adaptation process. Therefore, it is important for all the professionals who work with children who have disabilities to also have the skills necessary to carry out supportive counselling with their parents and other family members (Gargiulo, 1985; Seligman, 1979).

### 1.2.4 Linking parents with other parents

Surveys have shown that most parents want to meet others who have children with similar disabilities (Furneaux, 1988; Hornby, 1987). Whereas many parents wish to do this shortly after the diagnosis, some do not want such meetings for several months or even years. For example, one parent whom I met told me that although she was told about the relevant support groups when her daughter was diagnosed as having Down's syndrome, for the first few years she just wanted to treat her as normally as possible and therefore didn't want contact with any of the groups. After four years she joined a support group for parents of children with Down's syndrome and subsequently became very involved in the group's activities.

When parents do meet others who have children with similar disabilities they typically report great benefits both in terms of receiving emotional support and in obtaining information, such as about benefits available and respite care (Featherstone, 1981). Other family members, such as siblings and grandparents, also gain greatly from meeting with their peers from other exceptional families (Seligman and Darling, 1989). Professionals can help to facilitate these contacts by making families aware of the various support groups and other disability organizations operating in their area. They must realize that, even if parents don't make use of such groups immediately they will know of their existence for the future when they may be more interested and in need of the contact.

## 1.3 PROFESSIONAL KNOWLEDGE, ATTITUDES AND SKILLS

In order for practitioners to be able to fulfil the above functions and be of real help to parents and other family members they need to develop certain knowledge, attitudes and skills over and above the expertise associated with their own professions. In the final analysis it is the skills they use with parents which are the key, but unless these are grounded in the relevant knowledge and the appropriate attitudes, the effectiveness of their interventions will be limited.

### 1.3.1 Knowledge

Professionals should have a good understanding of the process which parents typically experience in coming to terms with the disability. When parents react to events with anger, denial or sadness, professionals should be able to be non-defensive and to help parents to work through their feelings, and thereby progress to a mature emotional acceptance of the child and his or her disability. Professionals should also have a thorough knowledge of the dynamics of such families and of the various factors both inside and outside families which influence their functioning. They should have an understanding of the likely effects of the disability on various members of the family, including siblings and grandparents. These aspects are discussed in Chapters 2 and 3.

Professionals should be aware of the various sources of additional finance which are available to parents including government benefits and grants from voluntary organizations. They need to be knowledgeable about the range of services which are available to parents and the agencies which supply them. They also need to be familiar with all other possible sources of help for families of children with disabilities, such as the parent support groups operating in the community where the family lives.

Finally, professionals should be knowledgeable about the different reactions to disability typical of different ethnic and cultural groups. They need to be sufficiently aware of the beliefs and customs of the ethnic groups with which they work to be able to adapt their interventions so that they are culturally appropriate.

### 1.3.2 Attitudes

The attitudes which professionals require in order to work effectively with parents are ones which are consistent with the development of a productive partnership. To bring this about professionals should possess the basic underlying attitudes of *genuineness, respect* and *empathy* suggested by Rogers (1980). They must be *genuine* in their relationships with parents. That is, they must come across as real people with their own strengths and weaknesses. For example, they should always be prepared to say that they 'don't know' when this is the case. In other words, they should relate to parents as people first and professionals second. Hiding behind a professional façade of competence is not in anyone's interest. Professionals should also show *respect* for parents. Parents' opinions and requests should always be given the utmost consideration. In the final analysis parents' wishes must be respected even if they run counter to the views of professionals, since it is parents who have the long-term responsibility for their children. Most importantly, professionals should develop *empathy* with parents. They should try to see the child and family's situation from the point of view of the parents. If professionals can develop an empathic understanding of the parent's position then it is likely that a productive parent–professional partnership will evolve.

Another important attitude which professionals need is to have hopeful but realistic views about the likely progress and eventual prognosis of the children with disabilities they work with. Parents need professionals to be optimistic but objective about their children's development. They need professionals to be people of integrity who will not shy away from being open and honest with parents but will do this with sensitivity. Professionals should also have a problem-solving orientation, that is, they need to be of the view that nothing is hopeless and that every situation can be improved, if perhaps not all of the problems can be completely solved.

### 1.3.3 Skills

In order to work effectively with parents professionals need good interpersonal communication skills. An essential part of this is the possession of basic listening and counselling skills. Several writers in the disability field have emphasized the importance of the use of such skills with parents (Seligman, 1979; Turnbull and Turnbull, 1986). Briefly, what is required is the ability to listen, understand, and help decide what action to take. Professionals must first of all listen to what parents have to say, in order to help them clarify their thoughts and feelings. Parents should then be helped to gain a clear understanding of the problem situation which they face or concern which they have. Finally, professionals should help parents decide what, if anything, they want to do about their problem or concern. That is, what action they wish to take. Possessing the skills required to implement this simple three-stage problem-solving model of counselling will contribute enormously to the ability of professionals to establish a productive working relationship with parents. The three-stage model and the skills which professionals need in order to use it are discussed in Chapters 5 and 6.

Other interpersonal skills required by professionals include the assertion skills needed for communicating effectively with parents and for collaborating with colleagues in the disability field. These are discussed in Chapter 7. In addition, professionals need group leadership skills so that they can organize various group experiences for parents. These skills are discussed in Chapter 8. Finally, the skills for empowering and enabling parents and for mentoring less experienced colleagues are required by professionals in order to promote the most effective parent–professional relationships. These skills are discussed in Chaper 9.

## 1.4 CONCLUSION

The remainder of this book is devoted to elaborating the skills, attitudes and knowledge which have been outlined above, in order to facilitate the development of these competencies in professionals who work with children with disabilities and their parents. The major focus of the book is on the interpersonal skills which professionals need in order to work effectively with parents. Therefore, it addresses the attitude and knowledge requirements relevant to the development of these skills. Other competencies related to working with parents are not specifically discussed because professionals are expected to have expertise in these areas as part of their own specialties and because there is already a substantial literature on these topics. Examples of the competencies not addressed, and of relevant texts, are: knowledge about the different disabilities (Batshaw, Perret and Carter, 1992; Bleck and

Nagle, 1975; Lansdown, 1980; Telford and Sawrey, 1981) and of the services available to parents (Furneaux, 1988; Philip and Duckworth, 1982; Stone and Taylor, 1977); coping with and helping to change attitudes towards people with disabilities (Fullwood and Cronin, 1986; McConkey and McCormack, 1983); and, practical skills, such as organizing individual and group meetings with parents (McConkey, 1985; Simpson, 1990).

## 1.5 SUMMARY

Becoming a parent of a child with a disability can happen to anyone. The experiences associated with the birth of the author's first child reinforced this and confirmed his opinion that a high level of interpersonal skills are needed by professionals in order to deal appropriately with parents whose child has been diagnosed as having a disability. It is proposed that the effectiveness of interventions with such children are dependent on professionals developing sound working relationships with the parents. Four essential functions of professionals in working with parents are considered to be: sensitively communicating diagnoses to parents; providing information about the disability and the services available; helping parents to come to terms with the disability; and, linking parents with others in similar situations. The skills, attitudes and knowledge needed by professionals in order to work effectively with parents are outlined as a precursor to their discussion in more detail in subsequent chapters.

The following chapter seeks to extend practitioners' knowledge of parental adaptation to disability and of the functioning of such families. Also discussed are the effects of disability on parents and other family members.

# 2

# Effects of disability on family members

## 2.1 INTRODUCTION

The impact of children with disabilities on parents and other family members has long been a concern of professionals and numerous books have been written on the subject over a period of almost thirty years (e.g. Chinn, Winn and Walters, 1978; Ross, 1964; Seligman, 1991). There is therefore a wealth of knowledge available to professionals about the likely effects of disability on such families.

Our understanding of relationships within families in general has grown considerably over this time and has moved on from early simplistic notions of powerful unilateral influences such as that suggested by maternal deprivation (Bowlby, 1965). Currently, families are viewed as interactive, interdependent systems with individual members reciprocally affecting each other, such that anything which affects one member of the family will have some impact on all other members and therefore on the family as a whole (Marshak and Seligman, 1993).

This change is reflected by a trend in the focus of research conducted with families who have children with disabilities.

In the 1950s, studies focused on the impact of parents on their children while in the 1960s they focused on negative effects on parents caused by their children. In the 1970s the impact on marital relationships and on siblings began to be studied. From the 1980s onwards research in this area has taken into account the interactive, interdependent nature of these families and much more complex views of how such families are affected by having a member with a disability have emerged (Bristol and Gallagher, 1986).

Given current views on the interactions within such families, an understanding of how these families function is necessary in order to gain an appreciation of the impact of having a child with a disability on parents and other family members. Therefore, in this chapter, the process of adaptation to the diagnosis of disability will be examined and there will be a consideration of various models used to describe the functioning of families which include children with disabilities. There will also be a discussion of the effects on family members, such as mothers, fathers, siblings and grandparents, of having a child with a disability.

## 2.2 ADAPTATION TO DISABILITY

Several models have been proposed to explain the process which people experience in adapting to a family member with a disability. Four of the most widely known models involve a continuum of stages of reaction, a series of developmental tasks, a number of existential crises, and, the experience of chronic sorrow. These are discussed below.

### 2.2.1 Stage model

Many writers (Bicknell, 1988; Gargiulo, 1985; Seligman, 1979) describe stage or phase models of adaptation to disability similar to the one developed by Hornby (1982) which is illustrated in Fig. 2.1 and described below. In this model, it is suggested that the process of adaptation can be viewed as a continuum of reactions, beginning at the diagnosis of disability, through which people pass in order to come to terms with the disabling condition.

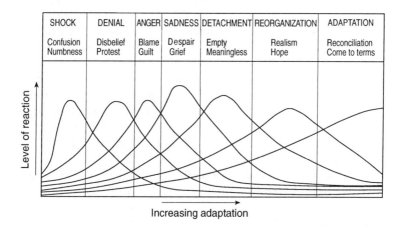

**Figure 2.1** Model of adaptation to disability.

The visual representation of the model of adaptation to disability, presented in Fig. 2.1, illustrates the continuum of stages of reaction beginning with shock and passing through denial, anger, sadness, detachment and reorganization until a state of adaptation to the disability has been reached. However, in reality, the adaptation process is not as clear cut as simply moving from stage to stage would suggest. The wavy lines representing the levels of reaction are there to demonstrate that although one reaction may be uppermost at a particular time, certain amounts of the other reactions involved in the process will also be present. For example, when parents' main reaction is one of anger they will also be experiencing a fair amount of denial and sadness at the same time, and lesser amounts of the other reactions will also be present. Sadness is shown as having the highest level of reaction because it is considered that feelings of sadness and grief are the overriding feelings and are ones which pervade all stages of the model more than any other.

### (a) Shock

The initial reaction of parents on being informed of their child's disability is typically one of shock. Parents report feeling confusion, numbness, disorganization and helplessness. Many parents say that they were unable to take in much of what they were told when the disability was diagnosed. One mother told me that when the paediatrician told her that her 18-month-old son had cerebral palsy she 'burst into tears' and didn't hear anything else. She had no idea what cerebral palsy was but she knew it wasn't good news. Another mother recounted how she had listened very calmly as the neurologist explained the extent of the brain damage her 14-year-old daughter had sustained as the result of a car accident. Then she got in her car and began to drive home, but after a few hundred yards, as she was crossing a bridge, she felt sick and her legs felt like they'd turned to jelly, so she got out of the car and leaned over the side of the bridge to get some air. Unfortunately, the bridge was one which many people had jumped off to commit suicide so she was quickly grabbed by passers by and a big fuss was created! Looking back she could see the funny side of the incident but at the time the shock reaction was clearly overwhelming.

The shock reaction usually lasts from a few hours to a few days. When this reaction has subsided parents are more able to take in information about the disability and are generally keen to learn as much as they can about the condition and what can be done to help. Therefore, professionals who communicate diagnoses to parents should be prepared to offer them a second interview a few days later in order to provide relevant information, as discussed in Chapter 1.

*(b) Denial*

Shock is typically followed by a phase characterized by denial or disbelief of the reality of the situation. At first, many parents find it difficult to believe that their child has a disability. They may think that there must have been a mistake. It is under-standable that they would want a second opinion and this option should be made available to them. However, for a few parents this leads to them 'shopping around' in an attempt to get a more favourable diagnosis, which, if found, will probably retard the adaptation process. This is why it is important that professionals are honest with parents and don't try to give them a prognosis which is too hopeful or unrealistic. Neither, of course, should they paint too bleak a picture. However, feedback from many parents has convinced me that the main qualities which they need from professionals at this time are accuracy and honesty. They want us to tell them exactly what we know and what we don't know. It is also very confusing for parents when professionals disagree about the diagnosis or prognosis and this can also reinforce their denial and retard the adaptation process.

As a temporary coping strategy denial is quite useful in giving parents time to adjust to the situation. It is only when denial is prolonged and intense that it is problematic. As the model suggests, some denial is present throughout the adaptation process and even when parents have apparently come to terms with the disability there may still be an element of denial present. Examples which come to mind include fathers of children with Down's syndrome who believe that their children can understand 'everything' that is said to them, it's just their 'speech that's the problem'; and the mother of a 12-year-old boy with Down's syndrome who told me that, even though she knew in reality that it would never happen, she still hoped that, 'one day he would come down the stairs and suddenly be normal'.

Professionals should therefore be sensitive to the degree which parents are using denial to cope with their reactions to the disability. Professionals can be of enormous help to parents in overcoming their use of denial. However, confronting the denial is seldom a useful strategy as it usually results in parents becoming anxious and rejecting the professional rather than accepting the reality of the disability. When denial is detected it is generally best to make greater use of listening skills while, at the same time, sensitively providing parents with objective information about their children's development and progress. In this way parents can be gradually helped to 'let go' of their denial.

### (c) Anger

Following denial, when parents are beginning to accept the reality of the situation, they tend to experience anger about the fact that their child has a disability. They may search for a cause of the disability, for someone to blame. If it appears that the disability occurred during the pregnancy or birth, then medical staff may be blamed and therefore may be on the receiving end of parents' anger. If not, there may be an investigation of the family histories of both parents to find out whether there have been other members of the extended family who have had a similar disability. If there is, then a parent's anger may be displaced onto their spouse. Alternatively, underlying the anger may be feelings of guilt about somehow being responsible for the disability. For example, if the disability has been caused by the rubella virus, then the parents may feel that they should have made sure that the mother had immunity before going ahead with the pregnancy.

It is important to realize that, whether parents are justifiably angry with professionals or not, anger is one of the reactions which most parents will experience as part of the adaptation process. They need to express this anger in order to move towards adaptation, so professionals should be willing to encourage parents to express and explore their angry feelings by using the listening skills discussed in Chapter 5.

### (d) Sadness

Sadness may follow anger and is a reaction which, more than any other, is reported to pervade the whole adaptation process. This sadness can be due to parents grieving for the loss of the healthy child which they expected or it can be due to sadness about the loss of opportunities and ambitions which their children will not be able to fulfil. Either way, sadness, depression and, in some cases even despair, are understandable reactions of parents to finding out that their child has a disability. Some parents have told me that they spent a lot of time crying. Others have reported that they felt so bad they couldn't face meeting anyone and tended to cut themselves off from social contact for quite a time.

It is important for professionals not to make assessments of parents' personalities based on their reactions of sadness or depression. This happened in one case I was involved in, when a mother's reaction to hearing about a second disability the child was discovered to have was considered to be evidence of clinical depression and was recorded as such in the child's file. Professionals need to realize that sadness and depression are a normal part of the adaptation process and parents must therefore not be labelled as depressive on the basis of experiencing this reaction for a period of time.

## (e) Detachment

Following sadness parents experience a sort of detachment, when they feel empty and nothing seems to matter. Life goes on from day to day but it has lost its meaning. The appearance of this reaction is considered to indicate that the parent has begun to reluctantly accept the reality of the disability. It is therefore thought to be a turning point in the adaptation process.

## (f) Reorganization

Reorganization is the reaction which follows detachment. It is characterized by realism about the situation and hope for the future. Parents begin to focus more on what their children may achieve and less on what they may miss out on.

When parents have reached this stage they are typically more interested in doing work with their children and participating in parent education programmes. So it is a good time for professionals to attempt to involve them in intervention programmes with their children and give parents the opportunity of attending parent programmes of various kinds. Being actively involved in facilitating their children's development and meeting up with other parents who have similarly disabled children often helps parents to feel better about the whole situation and therefore is useful in helping parents make progress towards adaptation.

## (g) Adaptation

Finally, parents are considered to reach a point when they have come to terms with the situation and exhibit a mature emotional acceptance of their child's disability. They are fully aware of the child's special needs and strive to provide for these. However, the child is treated, as much as possible, as just another member of the family, which does not revolve around him or her.

The adaptation process is considered to be a normal healthy reaction to the diagnosis of disability and can be viewed as a form of grieving similar to that which follows any traumatic loss, such as a bereavement (Kubler-Ross, 1969; Worden, 1983). Some parents appear to work through the process in a few days, whereas others seem to take years to reach a reasonable level of adaptation. Just as for any major loss it is considered that most people will take around two years to come to terms with a disability. However, some parents seem to take longer and a few possibly never fully adjust to the situation. For example, one father of a 12-year-old boy with Down's syndrome said to me, 'I still can't really believe he's my son'.

Passage through the adaptation process can be accelerated or retarded by what parents do and by what professionals say. Parents who refuse to face up to the disability and do not allow themselves to experience the feelings triggered by the adaptation process will take longer to come to terms with the situation. To use the terminology of grief therapy, parents need to do the 'grief work' associated with their loss in order to adjust to it (Worden, 1983). Professionals can also slow down parents' progress through the adaptation process by being insensitive and thereby reinforcing parents' anger which can then become a fixation, or by suggesting an unrealistic prognosis which often results in parents becoming stuck in the denial stage.

Some parents may partially work through the adaptation process in anticipation of the loss. The diagnosis of the disability is accompanied by feelings of relief for these parents. This appears to happen most often with parents of children with hearing impairment, who have had difficulty getting professionals to make a definite diagnosis, as is illustrated by the mother's story which is included in Chapter 3. I have also observed it fairly often in parents of children with specific learning difficulties, such as dyslexia, who are relieved to find out what is causing the child's problems at school.

In various surveys which have been conducted (Hornby, 1987; Wright, Granger and Sameroff, 1984) many parents have reported that they experienced feelings associated with more than one stage or phase at certain times. Some did not experience a particular phase, while others reported being fixated at one phase for a considerable time before being able to move on. Some people say that they experienced the phases in a different order. Thus, the process appears to be qualitatively different for each person.

This variability in people's responses has led some writers to question the accuracy of stage or phase models of adaptation (Allen and Affleck, 1985; Blacher, 1984). The major objections raised are theoretical difficulties in accepting a formal stage model with clearly defined stages and the lack of research evidence to support such a model. Therefore, it has been suggested that, rather than working through a continuum of reactions in order to come to terms with the disability, people are more likely to experience sadness or grief which may always be present to some extent.

### 2.2.2 Chronic sorrow

The above has led some writers to suggest that, rather than a grieving process which can be worked through with feelings to some extent resolved, parents of children with disabilities experience 'chronic sorrow' (Olshansky, 1962; Wikler, Wasow and Hatfield, 1981). It is suggested that the reactions which are evoked such as anger, sadness and denial are not resolved but become an integral part of the parents' emotional life (Max, 1985). Thus, there will be various occasions when these reactions may be re-experienced. This reworking of parental reactions can occur at various transition points in the disabled child's development, such as school entry, the onset of puberty, leaving school and leaving home (Wikler, 1981, 1986). It can also occur when parents are told about an additional disability at some time later than the original diagnosis. For example, Featherstone (1981) recounts how, having apparently come to terms with her child being blind, she was devastated when mental handicap was later diagnosed.

### 2.2.3 Existential conflicts

An alternative perspective on the adaptation process experienced by family members is provided by Roos (1963, 1978) who is a parent of a child with a disability as well as being professionally involved in the disability field. He suggests that, although people do experience the reactions discussed above to some extent, they may be more affected by various fundamental existential conflicts which are exacerbated by having a child with a disability. The existential conflicts identified by Roos include *disillusionment*. He considers that experience gradually erodes the high expectations which people develop as children, leading to disillusionment with ourselves, others, and life in general. Many people therefore channel their unrealistic expectations into their children. However a child with a disability is usually an unsuitable vehicle for fulfilling these expectations and therefore represents a major disillusionment.

Another conflict he calls *aloneness*. The fact that one is ultimately alone in one's passage through life is something that everyone must eventually come to terms with. Many people, however, attempt to avoid dealing with this conflict by establishing intimacy with their children. Since this is generally much more difficult with a child who has a disability, parents are often forced to face up to their existential loneliness. *Vulnerability* occurs because, as people mature they lose childhood fantasies of the omnipotence of their parents and themselves and begin to realize the tenuousness of their control over life, and therefore their personal vulnerability. Diagnosis of disability in a member of the family can be a painful reminder of this vulnerability.

*Inequality*, Roos suggests, occurs because children grow up with the notion that fairness and justice ultimately prevail in life. Therefore, when faced with a disability in the family, people may feel overwhelmed with the enormity of the apparent inequity, which can present a challenge to their ethical and religious beliefs. Also, maturity brings with it the realization of personal *insignificance*. Most people strive to find some meaning in life, perhaps through fulfilling satisfying social roles such as husband and father. When they are frustrated in achieving a rewarding parental role, because the child has a disability, people may find it difficult to achieve meaning in their lives and therefore become vulnerable to feelings of insignificance.

Another conflict Roos terms *past orientation*. Thus, while most parents anticipate their children's future with enthusiasm, parents of children with disabilities tend to view the future with apprehension. Hence, whereas most people are future oriented, such parents typically focus on the present or the past. Finally, he suggests that *loss of immortality* is another conflict. He explains that a common approach to coping with existential anxiety about one's own death is to seek symbolic immortality through one's children. When a child is disabled, however, this potential avenue to immortality is threatened. Particularly when the child is an only child, parents may be forced to face up to this existential conflict.

### 2.2.4 Developmental tasks

Yet another way in which the adaptation process can be viewed has been proposed by Mitchell (1985). Parents are seen as progressing through a series of developmental stages, each of which is characterized by a set of tasks which must be at least partially mastered if they are to successfully adapt to the presence of a disabled child in the family. Mitchell categorizes the tasks in four broad stages of development: initial diagnosis; infancy and toddlerhood; childhood and early adolescence; and, late adolescence and adulthood. The major tasks associated with each of these four stages are listed below.

(a) *Tasks associated with initial diagnosis:*

- deciding whether to pursue aggressive medical care
- deciding to keep the child or seek alternative care
- accepting the reality of the handicapping condition
- coming to terms with one's reactions to disability
- understanding the nature of the disability
- maintaining or enhancing self-esteem
- establishing a positive parenting relationship
- coming to terms with reactions of family and friends
- maintaining or enhancing relationship with spouse.

(b) *Tasks associated with infancy and toddlerhood:*

- making contact with other families of similar children
- accessing appropriate support services
- establishing working relationships with professionals
- coping with reactions of the broader community
- advocating for the rights of the disabled child
- establishing a balanced family and personal life

- developing skills for facilitating child's development
- coping with day to day tasks of caring for the child.

(c) *Tasks associated with childhood and early adolescence:*

- participating in decisions regarding special education
- maintaining working relationships with professionals
- accepting the prolonged dependence of the child
- facilitating adaptation of, and to, the community
- helping the child understand his or her disability.

(d) *Tasks associated with late adolescence and adulthood:*

- accepting the disabled person's right to independence
- accepting the disabled person's sexuality
- accepting disabled person living outside family home
- participating in decisions regarding jobs and training
- becoming familiar with the legal rights of the disabled
- ensuring future provision for disabled person.

It will be noted that many of these developmental tasks are ones which also apply to parents of non-disabled children (Havinghurst, 1972). However, knowledge of the specific tasks which apply to parents of children with disabilities enables practitioners to be aware of the kinds of issues which these parents may be dealing with, in addition to those of other parents, at various stages of the children's development.

### 2.2.5 Conclusions regarding models of adaptation

The major consideration at issue here is not so much whether adaptation of family members should be viewed as a continuum of emotional reactions, or characterized by chronic sorrow, or existential conflicts, or by stages of developmental tasks, but more that each model focuses attention on different aspects of the adaptation process. Each model is useful in providing insight into the lives of members of families with disabled children, thereby developing the understanding necessary for professionals to improve their working relationships with parents.

In my work, I have found the stage model of adaptation to be the most useful in raising professionals' awareness of parental reactions to disability. I have also found the stage model to be invaluable in working with parents. Parents benefit from knowing about the reactions they are likely to experience in coming to terms with their child's disability. Parents are often visibly moved when they are shown the stage model. On one occasion, which I remember, two mothers began to cry as I described the model to a group of parents. When I asked what had moved them so much they asked angrily why they had not been told about it earlier. They had been experiencing the re-actions described in the model and had thought they were perhaps going crazy! It was a tremendous relief for them to hear that such reactions are a normal part of the adaptation process.

Further understanding which professionals need to develop in order to work effectively with parents involves knowledge of the ways in which families function, which is discussed in the following section.

### 2.3 MODELS OF FAMILY FUNCTIONING

Three models of family functioning which have had an impact on work with families who have children with disabilities are the transactional model, the ecological model, and the family systems theory. These are described below.

#### 2.3.1 Transactional model

In this model development is believed to result from continual interplay between a changing organism and a changing environ-ment (Bell, 1968). Thus, families are considered both to be affected by their disabled members and to have an impact on them (Mink and Nihira, 1987). That is, the type and severity of the disability is likely to play an important role in how parents are affected and the kind of people parents are will have an important bearing on the child's behaviour and development. Also, as people with disabilities pass through different develop-mental stages they will affect their families in different ways. For example, an infant with a disability will have a different impact on parents than an adolescent with a similar condition. Like-wise, the effect parents have on their child with a disability will depend on the particular stage in the life cycle in which they find themselves. For example, a child who is the firstborn child of young, recently married parents is in a very different position to a child with the same disability born to older parents who already have several other children. The younger of these families is likely to experience higher levels of stress and have more difficulties in coping than the larger more established family.

### 2.3.2 Ecological model

This model suggests that human development and behaviour cannot be understood independently of the social context in which it occurs. The social environment influences behaviour and this occurs at several levels (Bronfenbrenner, 1977, 1979). Thus, the effects on parents of caring for a child with a disability are strongly influenced by the social environment in which they are living, including the extended family, services available and community attitudes. This is illustrated by the model, adapted from Mitchell (1985), which is presented in Fig. 2.2. The model includes four different levels of influence on the family: the microsystem, the mesosystem, the exosystem, and the macrosystem.

### (a) Microsystem

The family of a child with a disability is considered to constitute a microsystem with the child, parents and siblings reciprocally influencing each other. How well this nuclear family functions therefore depends on variables associated with each of its members. First, features of the disability itself such as the type, severity and when it was diagnosed will have an influence. For example, a disability such as Down's syndrome, which can be diagnosed at birth, can have a very different impact on the family to hearing impairment which is diagnosed later (as illustrated by the parents' accounts in Chapter 3). It is considered that a disability which is diagnosed early in the child's life is generally easier to come to terms with than one that is diagnosed later, since parents will have believed for several months or even years that the child was normal in every way and may find it difficult to change this belief. The severity of the disability is also an important factor. A child who is profoundly deaf is likely to have a different impact on the family to one who has a mild or moderate level of hearing impairment. Also, within the group of children who have

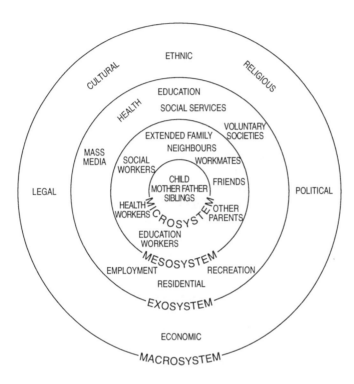

**Figure 2.2** Ecological model for the functioning of families of children with disabilities.

Down's syndrome there is a wide range of ability levels and frequent additional problems such as heart defects. A high functioning child with no additional problems is a very different prospect to one with life-threatening heart disease or profound mental handicap. Therefore, the impact on the family is likely to be quite different in each of these cases. Also, uncertainties about the diagnosis which often occur with disabilities such as dyslexia, autism and mild to moderate levels of learning difficulty can be more difficult for families to come to terms with than in clear cut cases such as Down's syndrome.

Second, factors associated with the child who has the disability and his or her siblings will have an influence on family functioning. Whether the child is the first born, last born, a middle child, an only child or a twin will have an impact on the family. The ages and personalities of children and their siblings will also play a big part in how well the family functions. A young baby with a disability can be cute whereas the same child as an adolescent whose behaviour is difficult to manage can have quite a different effect on the family. Older siblings can be resentful of the child with the disability and create problems of their own, or they can be helpful and make a substantial contribution to the family's well being. Younger siblings can create extra worries for parents who often feel that they are unable to pay them sufficient attention.

Third, factors associated with the parents themselves and their relationship will have a major influence on family functioning. The parents' ages, personalities, financial status, employment status, educational levels and the state of their health will all affect the family. For example, older parents are likely to have less financial worries than younger ones but may have more health problems of their own to worry about. Also, parents with extrovert personalities, who are optimistic and manage to keep a sense of humour will typically experience less stress than those who tend to dwell on the negative aspects of the situation they find themselves in. In addition, a key factor in the functioning of the nuclear family is the quality of the parents' marriage. A healthy marital relationship will exert a positive influence on the family whereas the consequences of an unhappy marriage are likely to be tension and conflict throughout the family microsystem.

### (b) Mesosystem

The family microsystem is influenced by the mesosystem in which it is embedded. The mesosystem comprises the range of settings in which the family actively participates, such as the extended family and the community in which the family lives. The extended family has a key role in determining how well parents cope with having a child with a disability. If extended family members, such as the child's grandparents, are understanding and supportive they can have a significant positive influence on family functioning, whereas if they are in conflict with the child's parents, or have little contact with them, the family misses out on an important potential source of support (as is illustrated by the parents' stories in the following chapter).

Neighbours, work mates, friends and other parents can also have a positive or negative influence on family functioning. When neighbours are friendly and allow the child with the disability into their homes to play with their own children parents can feel pleased that their family is accepted in the neighbourhood. If neighbours are unfriendly then this can put an added strain onto the family. In an extreme case, which I came across, the family had decided to move house because of the distress caused by neighbours who allowed their children to shout abuse at the child with Down's syndrome. Work mates and managers can also have an influence on the family. For example, managers who are prepared to give parents time off work to attend important appointments concerning their children can reduce parents' stress levels and thereby contribute positively to family well being. In contrast, work mates who talk of their own children's achievements while being too embarrassed to talk about the child with the disability turn a possible source of support into one of tension and unhappiness.

Typically, some of the parents' friends will find it difficult to adjust to them having a child with a disability and will tend to stay away. Parents themselves often shy away from many of their previous friends when they discover the disability (as is demonstrated in the father's story in the next chapter). This reduces the possible sources of support for the family. However, when parents meet up with other parents of children with similar disabilities they often form friendships which are very supportive and long-lasting. In many cases these friendships form an invaluable source of support for families, as is illustrated in the following chapter.

The contacts which parents have with, for example, social workers, teachers and doctors can help to promote healthy family functioning if these professionals are sensitive, understanding, knowledgeable and supportive. Parents of children with disabilities generally have a great deal of contact with professionals in the health, education and social welfare fields who can be an invaluable source of support and guidance, for example, regarding appropriate therapy, services and financial assistance. However, when parents find contacts with workers to be unhelpful, or even aversive, this increases stress and leads to reduced feelings of well being within the family.

### (c) Exosystem

The mesosystem is itself influenced by the exosystem which consists of social settings which indirectly affect the family, such as the mass media, education system and voluntary agencies. First of all, the way children with disabilities are portrayed in the newspapers or on television will have an impact on the family. When stereotyped and patronising attitudes toward people with disabilities are perpetuated by the media this does not help families who have disabled members to integrate into the community.

Second, the quality and types of health, education and social welfare services available to parents will have a critical influence on the way which these families cope with the disability. This is made clear when families with disabled children in developing countries such as India are considered. In many cases of severe disability such children do not attend school, no financial assistance is available to parents and medical attention is inadequate at best. Families in this situation will clearly find life very difficult indeed. Although the picture in Western countries, such as England, is generally much better, current political influences are forcing education, health and welfare services to operate like businesses. This is likely to have negative consequences for families of children with disabilities who typically need more intensive levels of help in these areas. For example, the availability of respite care for children with disabilities, so that families can have a break from time to time, is critical in helping many families cope. If the availability of this temporary care is reduced then this will have a negative impact on the functioning of many families.

Third, the availability of various voluntary societies and support groups which have been established to help the parents of children with disabilities can be a significant factor in determining how well these families cope. Involvement with such groups focusing on mental handicap and deafness had clearly become important parts of the lives of the father of a child with Down's syndrome and the mother of a child with hearing impairment whose stories are told in Chapter 3. In addition, both parents were also involved in providing help to other parents through a parent-to-parent scheme, the organization of which is described in Chapter 8.

Fourth, the availability of recreation facilities in the local community, suitable for the participation of children with disabilities is very important in helping families cope. This is particularly well demonstrated in Chapter 3 by the mother's account of her difficulties in finding suitable recreational activities for her daughter who is deaf. Recreational facilities can be set up especially for people with disabilities such as the PHAB group (physically handicapped able bodied) which organizes activities for physically disabled people with the help of non-disabled people. Alternatively, institutions such as sports and leisure centres can ensure that they provide appropriate access and programmes for people with disabilities. However, many parents find that recreational activities suitable for their children or young adults with disabilities in their local communities are inadequate which results in these young people being bored at home for much of their free time and an additional strain being put on the family.

Fifth, the employment and residential opportunities available for adults with disabilities have an indirect effect on how families function. One of the most frequently mentioned concerns of parents who have children with disabilities is anxiety about what will happen to their children in the future. In communities where there are various employment and residential options for adults with disabilities parents' worries are minimized. When this is not the case an enormous strain is placed on parents in attempting to find suitable work and living arrangements for when their children leave school.

### (d) Macrosystem

Finally, there is the macrosystem which refers to the attitudes, beliefs, values and ideologies inherent in the social institutions of a particular society, which all have an impact on the way a family of a child with a disability will function. First of all, the particular culture in which the family is living will have major effects on the family. If the culture is one which emphasizes humanitarian values then there is much more likely to be positive attitudes towards people with disabilities than in cultures which emphasize materialism. Also, the specific type of society in which the family lives will have an impact on many different aspects of family life. For example, if the family lives in a rural community in a developing country then it may be easier to prepare the disabled child for the types of work which are available than if the family lives in an urban community in an industrialized country.

The beliefs of the particular ethnic group to which the family belongs will exert an influence on the way the family reacts to the disability. For example, in traditional Samoan society having a disabled child in the family is thought to be the result of the father being unfaithful to his wife, so the child brings shame on the family. Religious beliefs also have a part to play in how families cope with having a disabled member. If the family believes the disabled child to be a gift of God then it will be much easier for them to accept the situation than if the disability is seen as a form of punishment for some sin which has been committed, as in the Samoan example mentioned above. Another example is that traditional Hindu families in India place far more store in going to the temple to make a gift to the Gods than they do in finding appropriate therapy for the child.

The overall economic situation in the society in which the family lives will affect many aspects of how the family copes with having a child with a disability. Typically, in developing countries, where there is insufficient money available to provide essential health and education services to the community, many of the facilities which are availabe for children with disabilities have been established by charitable organizations and a large proportion of disabled children do not receive appropriate health care, therapy or education. The professional guidance and financial support which is available to families in developed countries will also be mainly lacking, which adds to the difficulties experienced by these families.

In countries which are better off economically, political policies will be instrumental in determining how the resources are distributed. When economic policies are more concerned with increasing profits than with improving the quality of life of the citizens, then people with disabilities and their families are likely to do less well. The political system in each country is responsible for the legislation regarding the rights of children with disabilities and their families. The legal system has a role to play in interpreting the law in terms of individual cases of people with disabilities. However, these cases typically indirectly affect large numbers of similar families since the legal rulings are often used to provide guidance for services in the health, education, and social welfare fields. Recent years have witnessed increasing use of the legal systems in countries such as the USA and the UK, by parents attempting to ensure their children with disabilities receive the best possible services. The ability to engage in such a process is clearly important in determining the levels of support available to such families.

In conclusion, it must now be clear that how a family with a disabled member functions is influenced, not only by interactions within the family's microsystem but also by its interactions with other levels of the entire social system, which all must be taken into account by professionals when they are working with children with disabilities and their families.

### 2.3.3 Family systems theory

This model suggests that the behaviour of family members is a function of the family system of which they are a part (Berger and Foster, 1986; Foster and Berger, 1985). A change in the family system will inevitably lead to a change in the behaviour of each of the family members. Likewise, a change in an individual's behaviour will cause the family system to change. However, the functioning of the family system is considered to comprise more than just a summation of the contributions of its individual members. Interactions between family members and the organizational structure of families also play a part in family dynamics. Intervention at the level of the family system is therefore likely to have more impact than intervention aimed at one of its members (Berger, 1984; Coopersmith, 1984).

An illustration of the application of systems theory comes readily to mind. I have been attempting to convince my wife of the importance of considering the whole family system in doing the best for our young son. This lucky young man has been getting the very best fresh foods such as, sweet potato, plantain and paw paw, individually cooked especially for him by his mother while his parents have been surviving mainly on frozen packet food from the supermarket! The many hours taken by my wife in preparing these meals for the baby naturally detracts from the time available for her to spend doing things for herself and, more importantly, doing things with and for her husband! Seriously, this issue has highlighted how much the arrival of our son has changed the interactions and the structure of what is now our nuclear family. It has brought home to me how much children, mothers, fathers and marital relationships all need attention if families are to function well. It has also reminded me how paying a disproportionate amount of attention to one family member can unbalance the family and create problems. Therefore, I'm even more convinced that a family systems perspective is invaluable for professionals in the health, education and social welfare fields. Surprisingly, however, my explanation of family systems theory has not resulted in a drastic change in my wife's cooking priorities!

In contrast to a family systems perspective, many practitioners in the disability field consider themselves to be working with individual clients quite independently of their families and believe that this work will only affect the children or adults directly involved. However, the implication of family systems theory is that intervention with a person with a disability will have an impact on the whole family to which that person belongs. Therefore, the whole family system needs to be taken into account when considering the effects of an intervention on an individual family member. Some writers go as far as to suggest that an intervention with any family member is in fact an intervention with the whole family (Berger and Foster, 1986). Others go even further and claim that treatment of individuals, without taking their families into account, may result in an increase in problems experienced by the family as a whole (Chilman, Nunnally and Cox, 1988).

A knowledge of family systems theory provides an excellent rationale for practitioners working with families of children with disabilities to always consider the child's family and where possible involve family members, typically parents, in the treatment programmes. In order to help practitioners work effectively with such families a conceptual framework for understanding family systems has been developed. This is discussed next.

## 2.3.4 Family systems conceptual framework

This framework was developed by Turnbull and her associates in order to elucidate the various elements of the family system with particular relevance to children with disabilities (Turnbull, Summers, and Brotherson, 1984; Turnbull and Turnbull, 1986). The framework is made up of four components: family interaction, family resources, family functions, and family life-cycle. These are discussed below.

### (a) Family interaction

This component refers to the relationships that occur within and between the various sub-systems of family members. That is, the spousal sub-system (husband–wife interactions), the parental sub-system (parent–child interactions), and the sibling sub-system (child–child interactions). It also refers to extra-familial interaction such as those between children and grandparents or those between a father and his work mates.

It has been suggested that professionals should be cautious about intervening within a sub-system (Marshak and Seligman, 1993). For example, interventions which are likely to strengthen a mother's relationship with the child may have negative implications for the father's relationship with the child and for the marital relationship. Wherever possible, interventions should involve both parents and perhaps also involve older siblings.

Other aspects of family interaction are *cohesion, adaptability* and *communication*. The two extremes of *cohesion* are enmeshment and disengagement. Enmeshed families have weak boundaries between sub-systems and therefore tend to be overprotective of the child with the disability whereas disengaged families have rigid sub-system boundaries and exhibit a lack of care for each other and neglect of the child. A healthy family functions somewhere between these two extremes such that the disabled child feels cared for but is encouraged to be as independent as possible. *Adaptability* refers to the family's ability to change in response to events. The more inflexible family members are the more difficulties the family will face in adapting to living with a child with a disability. *Communication* refers to the communication patterns within the family. This suggests that professionals should focus on changing patterns of interaction within the family not on an individual's communication difficulties.

### (b) Family resources

This component consists of descriptive elements of the family, including characteristics of the disability such as type and severity; characteristics of the family such as size, cultural background and socio-economic status; and personal characteristics such as health, ideologies and coping styles. The impact of these factors on the family system have been discussed in relation to the microsystem level of the ecological model described earlier in this chapter.

### (c) Family functions

This component refers to the different types of needs for which the family provides such as economic, physical care, recuperation, socialization, affection, self-definition, educational and vocational needs. All families differ regarding the priorities they attach to the various functions and with respect to which family members are assigned to perform specific roles within the family. However, caring for a member with a disability is likely to affect these family functions in certain ways. For example, the family's earning capacity may be reduced because one parent is unable to work due to the extra demands placed on the family. Also, the career aspirations of the parent who works may be constrained by the family's need to live in a particular area in order to obtain the best possible services or schooling for their disabled child (this is illustrated by the parents' stories which are told in the following chapter). In addition, restrictions are likely to be placed on the family's social and recreational activities. Finally, the family's self-definition, or the way members view themselves and their family are likely to be changed when a child with a disability becomes part of the family (Marshak and Seligman, 1993).

### (d) Family life-cycle

This component represents the sequence of developmental changes that affect families as they progress through various stages in the life-cycle, such as unattached adulthood, marriage, birth of children, school entry, adolescent children, children leaving home, and retirement. Also, within the family life-cycle, the individual life-cycles of each of the family members need to be considered. For example, Levinson (1978) has suggested that adult males traverse a life-cycle consisting of early adulthood, mid-life transition, middle adulthood, late adult transition, and late adulthood. Each family member is therefore engaged with developmental tasks associated with the relevant stages in the family life-cycle and their own individual life-cycle. In most cases individual and family tasks would be similar but when parents have children later in life or have children from a previous marriage things become more complicated (Carter and McGoldrick, 1980).

Children with disabilities will be slow to develop in some areas and therefore have life-cycles which differ from those of their siblings. This is likely to create conflict within the family at various stages. For example, the family life-cycle stage of children leaving home is likely to be delayed or blocked totally because the family is not willing or able to find a suitable living arrangement outside the home for the disabled member. This then frustrates other family members, usually the parents, from progressing with developmental tasks necessary to fulfil their own life-cycle demands, such as preparing for retirement.

Finally, in addition to considering the likely effects of individual and family life-cycle factors, it must be remembered that these life-cycle variables affect family functions and resources, which in turn affect family interaction patterns. These four components of the family system are considered to be interdependent, which means that a knowledge of all four components of the family system is needed when considering the impact of any event on an individual member of the family. In the USA legislation has been enacted which specifically requires pre-school programmes to use a family systems model in their interventions with children with disabilities and their families. From a family systems perspective, the goals of any intervention are to identify the family's needs and resources, locate the services and support required for meeting those needs and help families to access these (Dunst, Trivette and Deal, 1988). Professionals therefore need to use their knowledge of the family systems conceptual framework in planning interventions for the children with disabilities with whom they work.

## 2.4 EFFECTS ON FAMILIES AND THEIR MEMBERS

The importance of considering the effects on families due to one of their members having a disability has been increasingly realized in recent years. Whereas most of the existing literature refers to effects on parents, the vast majority of research has been conducted with mothers. Comments about fathers, siblings and other family members have often been gained from surveys conducted with mothers, whose perceptions of the reactions of other family members may not always be accurate. With this reservation in mind, the extensive literature regarding the effects on such families and their members will now be briefly reviewed.

### 2.4.1 Families

The social life of many families with disabled members is likely to be restricted (Lonsdale, 1978; Philip and Duckworth, 1982). Leisure activities such as participation in sports and other clubs and family activities, such as visiting friends, having picnics and attending family gatherings, are often affected. Many families are restricted in the use they can make of community facilities such as beaches, restaurants and public transport. There are also limitations in the type of holidays which families can take. The extent of the social restriction is greatest when the children are young, when physical handicap or behavioural problems are present and when the degree of handicapping condition is severe (Gallagher, Beckman and Cross, 1983).

Families who have children with disabilities are also likely to have to meet additional expenses (Lonsdale, 1978; Murphy, 1982). These are most often for medical care, clothing and transport. The family's income may also be reduced since one parent is prevented from going out to work because of the daily care requirements of the disabled child (McAndrew, 1976). Most countries have various financial benefits available to assist such families. However, surveys have shown that many parents do not receive the benefits to which they are entitled (Hornby, 1987; Philip and Duckworth, 1982).

## 2.4.2 Marriage

Much has been written concerning the potential marital difficulties faced by parents of children with disabilities (e.g. Featherstone, 1981; Max, 1985). These difficulties are considered to be related to the additional demands of caring for a child with a disability, and various other factors. It is suggested that spouses may disagree about the child's care or treatment and have insufficient time to resolve their conflicts. Having to deal with several professionals may increase the strain on parents, particularly since it is usually the mother who sees the professionals, and who has to re-interpret the meetings for the father. It has also been suggested that, because of greater involvement with professionals, and the child, mothers sometimes move through the adaptation process more quickly than fathers, creating another area for conflict. Difficulties in sexual relationships may result from a lack of privacy, fatigue, a sense of isolation on the part of each spouse, or the fear of producing another disabled child (Featherstone, 1981).

Several studies have investigated the prevalence of marriage breakdown in such families. Overall, the results have been inconclusive, with reports of high marriage breakdown and low marital satisfaction (Gath, 1977; Murphy, 1982; Tew, Payne and Lawrence, 1974) being balanced by findings of average levels of marital satisfaction and breakdown in other studies (Furneaux, 1988; Gath and Gumley, 1984; Roesel and Lawlis, 1983). One result which has been consistently found is that a stable and satisfying marriage appears to reduce the stress experienced by parents in coping with a disabled child (Gallager, Beckman and Cross, 1983; Minnes, 1988). These findings have led some researchers to suggest that having a child with a disability in the family tends to strengthen strong marriages and weaken fragile ones (Brotherson *et al.*, 1986).

## 2.4.3 Mothers

Many studies have shown that the bulk of the housework and child care in families with disabled members is carried out by mothers (Fewell and Vadasy, 1986; Parke, 1986). Despite the increased demands which a disabled person makes on these aspects of family life fathers generally do not make a bigger contribution than they make in ordinary families (Gallagher, Scharfman and Bristol, 1984; McConachie, 1986). Another fairly consistent and probably related finding is that mothers of disabled children exhibit higher levels of stress than mothers of non-disabled children (Minnes, 1988). Some studies have reported that this has led to such mothers suffering a higher incidence of stress-related physical and mental disorders than mothers in ordinary families (Gallager, Beckman and Cross, 1983; Philip and Duckworth, 1982).

### 2.4.4 Fathers

Besides generally playing a smaller part than mothers in the day-to-day care of their disabled children most fathers also have less contact with professionals. These factors may lead to fathers experiencing greater difficulties than mothers in coming to terms with their disabled children. Alternatively, since fathers go off to work during the day and generally have other interests outside the home their mental health may be less threatened than that of mothers. However, fathers are often said to use denial to avoid facing up to the full extent of the disability or to hide their true feelings about the situation (Featherstone, 1981).

In fact, the overall impression gained from the literature about effects on fathers of parenting children with disabilities, is generally a negative one (Hornby, 1994). Fathers are reported to have difficulty in accepting the disability, particularly if it occurs in a son or if the child is severely handicapped (Lamb, 1983). Also, fathers are reported to experience a higher level of depression, personality difficulties and marital relationship problems than fathers of non-disabled children (Brotherson *et al.*, 1986; Meyer, 1986 a, b). However, a recent study has found that there is little evidence for these negative effects on fathers (Hornby, 1993, 1994). The one hundred fathers of children with Down's syndrome, who were interviewed and completed questionnaires, were found not to differ significantly from other fathers on the variables studied such as stress, depression, personality factors and levels of marital satisfaction.

## 2.4.5 Siblings

Much has been written about the possible harmful effects on the siblings of children with disabilities. Seligman and Darling (1989) suggest that there are several factors which can contribute to sibling maladjustment. Siblings may be given excessive caretaking responsibilities or may feel the need to overachieve to compensate for parental disappointment with the disabled child. Children may also wonder whether parents will expect them to care for their disabled sibling in later life and may worry about finding a spouse who would be willing to share such a responsibility (Featherstone, 1981). Other concerns are anxiety about 'catching' the disability or about the future possibility of producing handicapped children themselves (Crnic and Leconte, 1986; Simeonsson and McHale, 1981).

There are, however, several reports of the positive effects on sibling adjustment of having a disabled family member. One example of this is that many siblings are reported to choose careers in the helping professions such as teaching or social work (Furneaux, 1988). Other researchers have suggested that siblings of children with disabilities tend to be more insightful and tolerant of others' difficulties, to be more certain of their goals in life, to demonstrate greater social competence, and to develop a maturity beyond their years (Crnic and Leconte, 1986; Ferrari, 1984; Grossman, 1972).

## 2.4.6 Grandparents

A common source of support for the family may be the disabled child's grandparents. Grandparents can provide emotional support, guidance about child care, access to community resources, as well as help with shopping, baby-sitting and financial support (Sonnek,1986; Vadasy, Fewell and Meyer, 1986). However, some reports have suggested that many grandparents have difficulty adapting to the situation and either attempt to deny the reality of the handicap or reject the child (George, 1988; Seligman and Darling, 1989). Another reported problem is the paternal grandmother's resentment of her daughter-in-law for not producing a normal child (Pieper, 1976). These difficulties can lead to a breakdown in the relationship between parents and grandparents, which is then likely to have a pervasive effect on family members. In fact, a recent survey of parents of children with severe learning difficulties found that there was a low level of support from grandparents (Hornby and Ashworth, 1994). A minority of grandparents provided a high level of support and more support was received from maternal grandparents than paternal grandparents but generally grandparents were found to provide minimal support for the families caring for their disabled grandchildren.

## 2.5 SUMMARY

Professionals working with children with disabilities need to be aware of the likely impact of caring for such children on members of their families. An understanding of the process by which parents and other family members adapt to a disability is therefore essential. Four models for the adaptation process have been discussed. These involve the adaptation process being viewed as a continuum of stages of reaction, a series of developmental tasks, a number of existential crises, or the experience of chronic sorrow. Also essential is an understanding of the ways in which these families typically function. Therefore, four models of family functioning have been presented. These are: the transactional model, the ecological model, family systems theory, and the family systems conceptual framework. Finally, the typical effects of childhood disability on families, mothers, fathers, siblings, grandparents and the marital relationship are briefly discussed. It is proposed that if professionals are to establish productive working relationships with parents then they need to have a comprehensive knowledge of the issues addressed in this chapter.

In order to provide examples of these issues in practice, the following chapter recounts the personal stories of two parents who have children with different types of disabilities.

# 3

# Two parents' stories

## 3.1 INTRODUCTION

In order to illustrate the various models and issues discussed in the previous chapter, the focus of the current chapter is on parents' perspectives of the effects of their children with disabilities on themselves and their families. There are now numerous books and articles written by parents themselves about their experiences. Many of these provide excellent insight into the impact of disability on families (e.g. Featherstone, 1981; Hannam, 1988). However, in a recent review of material produced by fathers (Hornby, 1992a) it was found that these writers were not representative of fathers of children with disabilities in general, as the majority were highly educated and came from upper middle class families. Further, these fathers' accounts painted an overwhelmingly negative picture of the impact of disability on themselves and their families. This was in stark contrast to the much more balanced picture obtained from a recent study in which a hundred fathers of children with Down's syndrome were surveyed (Hornby, 1933, 1994).

It is likely that mothers who have written books about their experiences of parenting children with disabilities are similarly unrepresentative. Many books by mothers seem to be organized around a theme of how much their child has achieved despite a lack of appropriate help from professionals (e.g. Browning, 1987; Hebden, 1985)! However, there are other books which provide a more balanced picture (e.g. Featherstone, 1981; Thompson, 1986).

In order to present a balanced perspective in this chapter it was decided to obtain material from interviews conducted with two parents who the author knew personally through their participation in parent-to-parent schemes in New Zealand (Chapter 8) and who were considered to be able to present a more typical picture of parents' experiences.

The parents selected were the mother of a 12-year-old girl with profound hearing impairment and the father of a 5-year-old girl with Down's syndrome. They were first contacted by telephone and when they agreed to the interviews were sent a list of the topics to be covered. These were:

- how they and other family members found out about the disability and reacted to the news;
- what had the process of adjustment been like for them and other family members;
- what were the effects on family members, their marriage and themselves;
- what sources of support did they have and how had they found them;
- what made coping more difficult or had been unhelpful;
- what concerns had they currently and for the future;
- what advice had they for professionals and parents.

Both parents were interviewed at home. During the interview they were encouraged to tell their own stories using the above topics as a guide. The parents were asked to elaborate on any opinions and to focus on any feelings which they expressed. The interviews were tape recorded and were later transcribed. All names were changed to protect anonymity in line with parents' wishes. The names of the local agencies which parents referred to were also changed so that an international readership could understand what type of service was being referred to.

## 3.2 ACCOUNT BY A MOTHER OF A 12-YEAR-OLD GIRL WITH PROFOUND HEARING IMPAIRMENT

We have three children. There are two boys, the eldest one, David, is 15. Michael is almost 13. Then there is Joanne who is 12. She is profoundly deaf. We adopted Joanne, the boys are ours. We had a baby that died, another boy. After that we decided to adopt a girl. It was easier 12 years ago to adopt than it is today and we were lucky enough to get Joanne.

Before she was 3 months old we felt there was something wrong with her hearing. I used to put her on the floor to do her exercises. We have always had big dogs and one day, I remember particularly, the dog barked behind her and she stayed there. Anybody else would have jumped but she did not and that was the first time it occurred to me that she had not heard. As I was taking her to the doctor shortly afterwards, for her immunization, I mentioned to him that I was a bit concerned about this. He told me that I was an over-anxious adoptive mother and implied that I was being ridiculous about the whole thing. It knocked my confidence somewhat. I didn't do anything further and just generally watched her over the months, but the more I did my own tests the more I was positive there was a problem.

She is a very bright little girl, always has been. If you stood behind her she would turn around to see what you were doing. People would say, 'Of course she can hear', because she turned around. So I became rather confused about the whole thing myself, wondering whether I was getting a bit too anxious. By the time she was 9 months old, I was in such a state I had to know but it didn't occur to me at the time to take myself off to an Ear, Nose and Throat (ENT) specialist. When I went to the health visitor for the 9 months check I knew that she would do a hearing test and I spoke to her about the problem I was having with Joanne. She did the test and once again Joanne looked around to see what she was doing. The health visitor said that she didn't think there was a problem. I promptly burst into tears and said, 'What am I going to do? I know there is something wrong with this child but nobody will believe me'. So I think just to keep me happy she said she would get me an appointment wih an audiologist. Nothing happened for quite some time until they phoned me one day, about two months later, and asked why I had not come. I said I was still waiting for the appointment, so they ticked me off because, apparently, they had sent one in the mail and I didn't receive it. So with one thing and another Joanne wasn't actually tested until she was a year old. When the assessment was finally done it came out that she was profoundly deaf, so at least I knew I had been right all along. In fact, I was quite relieved because once I knew for certain what was wrong with her I could go on and find out what could be done for deaf children.

When the audiologist diagnosed Joanne as being profoundly deaf my husband was with me. He's very good and always comes if there is anything important like that, because obviously he was concerned too. I was glad that he was with me and it also made me realize that the professionals who tell parents about their children's disabilities need to be very tactful, very sensitive people. I would imagine that a lot of parents are very distraught and would need time to accept the diagnosis, though this wasn't the case for me. Also, I think there should be a follow-up visit so that parents can go away and accept the fact or discuss it with their partner and family because when you are told these things you don't always absorb everything you are told. You need time to go home and think about it. Life is obviously going to be different from now on. All sorts of questions come up so I think you should have a set time of maybe two weeks before having another visit to that same person who has told you about your child, so that you can ask questions which you hadn't thought of at the time. I would like to have asked about the causes and type of deafness Joanne had, and what possibilities there were at the time. Also, I would have liked to have known more about the education of deaf children and been able to talk to somebody who could tell me what sort of future there was for her. Also, I now know of mothers' groups, which I wasn't told about until a couple of years later. I would have liked another parent that I could get in contact with, with a child perhaps a little older, to give me some idea of what was ahead in bringing up a deaf child. Going back to the audiologist at a later date would have been very helpful to find out about the workings of audiograms, which I was shown at the first meeting and didn't understand at the time.

Also, I would like to have spoken to the audiologist about the medical side of deafness and asked what possible future there was for any improvement, operation-wise. At that time we were very confused and needed to discuss these things.

Some time after the initial visit to the audiologist, a professional concerned with deaf children came to see us. I asked questions and found out quite a lot from her about the education of deaf children. She gave me lots of advice on how to encourage my child to speak and how to make her watch me and develop. But she didn't tell me about the mothers' group and I didn't think to ask to be referred to another parent. I felt that we were pretty isolated but I didn't know how to go about getting out of the isolation.

Once I knew that Joanne was deaf I read a lot of library books, anything to do with deafness, and there was one book that mentioned the John Tracy Clinic, and the correspondence course. So I wrote away for that and found it helpful because I could write and get out of my system any frustrations that I had. Also, they gave me quite a few ideas about games for Joanne. However, a lot of books deal only with the deaf child without considering the whole family. This is the fault with a lot of them, that they don't include the effect of having a deaf child on the whole family and I think that is very important.

Regarding my family, when Joanne was born I already had two children. The two boys are not a great deal older than Joanne so they were always used to her and all grew up together. My husband accepted it pretty well because I did and he tends to follow my lead. I think perhaps if I hadn't been able to handle the situation he might have found it very difficult. But he has always been very supportive. If I have needed to go to the ear specialist or the audiologist or anywhere in particular he would always try and come with me.

As the children have become older my boys find Joanne can be very difficult at times because she has a different kind of personality. They are rather gentle boys whereas she is very outgoing and very active. She is really slightly overactive in that she needs constant activity. She can be bossy and noisy and they find over long periods that this can be very irritating. Also, there is definitely a stress on the family with the constant noise level. I was always told to let her talk, which I did and she does talk non-stop whenever possible. I have to stop her so that we can talk ourselves. But it's practically unintelligible language, very difficult to understand. There is a constant strain of concentrating on what she is saying. Being able to answer her so that she understands is also a constant thing in our family. All of us have to be able to do this. If I am talking to one of the boys and she interrupts me then I will say, 'Wait, I am talking to David', and I will finish the conversation first.

I think it is important to give your time to the other children, not only to the handicapped child. That has been very difficult because, especially in the pre-school years, I worked very hard with Joanne and considered her a lot. I took the children out a lot more than I would have because I realized she needed experiences. You had to be doing and seeing, therefore we went out a lot, to all sorts of different places. Even now, on holidays, we do different things. One holiday we will go to a farm, another holiday we will go up to the snow. She needs to see, to feel, to smell because she can't hear conversation about these things and therefore can't visualize them; she needs to actually see them herself. However, the boys have different interests and I have to take that into consideration too.

As to the impact on the wider family, my parents are divorced and they don't live in this country. They do come and visit me every now and again and I think that they really find Joanne very difficult to handle. My mother, who lives overseas, does send me articles on deaf children but she finds Joanne very difficult when she comes to visit me. She doesn't understand that she is inquisitive and needs to see things. For example, as a pre-schooler Joanne went through her handbag to see what was there. My mother thought that she was being rude and nosy, whereas in actual fact she was curious to know what somebody kept in their handbag. I was also taught myself to be seen and not heard and now my family is fairly noisy because of Joanne. So my mother finds this very difficult and I think if she lived with us she would find it intolerable. My husband's parents were much older and they found Joanne very difficult also. I had no support from family. My sister lives overseas so I see her very rarely. My husband's brother lives in the same city as us but he has his own family and there is not much communication. So we are a very isolated unit.

We have a lot of very good friends and I have found that those friends are more supportive than our family. Right from the beginning, when I knew for sure Joanne was deaf, I met a deaf lady who took her children to the same kindergarten to which I was taking my boys. When I saw that she was wearing a hearing aid I approached her, asked her if she was deaf, and told her I had a deaf daughter. We became very good friends and still are. She's opened up the adult deaf world to me which I have found very helpful because I can see that Joanne will grow up like those people and will be able to do anything that they do, driving cars, getting married, having babies and all the positive things that the deaf adult can do. I needed to know how Joanne was going to grow up. So having her to refer to and to be able to ask her questions was really very, very, good support.

Once I realized that there was a weekly mothers' club meeting at the special school for deaf children which Joanne attends, I went to that regularly. Then when Joanne went to a pre-school for deaf children I became very close to other parents of those children. The group of us became very close. In fact, from then on we went on outings together with our deaf children and we keep in contact now as the children grow. That is very supportive, because our children are now 12 years old and starting to go through puberty with all the problems you have there, such as behavioural problems and the girls wanting pretty clothes and wanting to shave their legs and use deodorants and so on. It is great to compare notes and find out that others are doing the same thing and to know that it is quite normal. So I find that it is excellent to have these parents to talk to.

As to professionals, I do have difficulties at times with my GP. I am very sensitive, obviously, to any ear problems that Joanne might have. She has a little hearing, in only one ear, so I need to protect that. So if she gets infections of any sort I am on the doctor's doorstep like a shot. He's a very good doctor in that he doesn't like to give out antibiotics unless essential. But on the other hand he doesn't understand my concern. Maybe it's over-concern but I think I'm justified and there have been times when I have had to go over his head and take Joanne to the ENT specialist who has always been very accessible to us. At one stage Joanne had very bad tonsillitis. Our GP said she had an allergy which I knew was incorrect. I was able to go to the ENT specialist and he was very supportive and said to come if I ever needed to. He understood my need and gave her antibiotics there and then. So I have very good backup from him. Also he keeps me informed of any medical advances. We have discussed the fact that unless something becomes very advanced Joanne will never be able to have any improvement to her hearing because of her nerve deafness. I accept that.

Regarding professionals in the field of deafness, the only persons we have seen have been the advisers on deaf children who work in the education service, and in the early days not often enough. The first year I saw the adviser fairly regularly, about once a month, and she was extremely helpful to me which was great. I think it was the second or third year when I saw the adviser only twice for a whole year and one of those times she only popped in briefly. She didn't have time to see Joanne or spend time with her because she had spent more time with the previous child. They were very understaffed at that time, but I felt from a parent's point of view I needed the contact and needed to be helped along because Joanne was growing so quickly and needed to be extended to her full ability.

One difficulty we have had has been with the respite care scheme which is organized to give parents a break. We had difficulty getting ours. I put in an application form, filled out by the GP. Then we received a letter saying it hadn't been approved and that we were not eligible. I was very angry about that. I had got to the stage where I needed to have that break – not having family near to leave my children with I needed to have a break. So I went with my husband to the social services department and we spoke first to the girl at the desk. Then spoke to another lady and didn't get anywhere. So I said we wanted to speak to the director, and we stayed until we saw him. When he came I said, 'Can you tell me why we have not been accepted?' After a lot of assertion on my part he pointed out that the doctor had filled in the sentence which said to the effect, 'Did this child need full supervision', and the GP had written 'No', and this was apparently what it had been assessed on. I tried to explain the difficulties in having a deaf child in the family and the strain it causes and he said

'Do you go to a specialist?' and I said 'Yes'. Then he told us to get another form and ask the specialist to fill it out, which I did. The specialist wrote in quite a lot of detail. This time it was accepted. So we got our break, our holiday with the other children, which was very much needed. It was quite an upsetting thing, to be refused something we felt was our right as parents of a handicapped child. It was just a little bit of help and we hadn't used it before.

Another difficulty which we had was due to a disagreement I had over teaching Joanne. After reading a lot of books on deafness I came to the conclusion that deaf people needed to use their eyesight to compensate for the lack of hearing. So I used my own sign language, which is very simple. I mentioned this to the adviser and she told me that I must teach Joanne to lip read and to speak. She suggested that I sit on my hands! I disagreed, although at the time I didn't actually say so. I was quite surprised that she should say this to me. I continued to use those signs until in later years sign language became accepted by the Education Department. Obviously I had been doing the right thing. I did tell her that I would teach my child to finger spell so that I would know whether she was spelling correctly. I was uncomfortable the next time the adviser came. I didn't tell her that I was still using my signs. I felt a bit sneaky about doing it but I felt in my heart that I was doing the right thing.

Another difficult area has been Joanne's leisure time. I thought it would be very nice for her to join normal activities that little girls of her age would do, for example, girls brigade. That was the first organization that we encouraged Joanne to go to. They are very church orientated. They gave her prayers and made her recite hymns of which she had no comprehension at all. She had no idea what it was all about and they were unable to explain things to her, so she became very bored with that group and I withdrew her from that, and from Sunday school. So that now, when my husband and the boys go to church on Sundays Joanne and I do things together.

The second organization I took her to was Brownies, and she knew quite a few little girls that went. Unfortunately the leaders weren't exactly frightened of her but they didn't like to try and communicate with her. If they wanted her to come they would send one of the children to go and get her. They were unable to explain anything to her, such as stories they were reading, so she became very bored. They tended to ignore her. I did go along several times but I felt that she needed to go to these things by herself. She didn't want me always tagging along behind, but unless I went with her she missed out on activities.

She is a very active child and I'm very interested in horse riding myself. I took her to our local pony club and asked if perhaps we could join the club. They said that would be alright but I would have to come and interpret for her and that I could have a couple of trial sessions, which I did. I found the instructors would stand in the middle of the group of children and ponies and yell instructions at her which she was too far away to lip read and without hearing she didn't understand what they wanted. They suggested that it was no good bringing her to the pony club.

The next group which she joined was the guides, mainly because in my work I had contact with the local commissioner for the guides who is partially deaf herself and suggested a small group of guides would be a lot more considerate of her condition, a lot more helpful. By this time I was getting a bit upset about the whole thing thinking that she would never be able to do the normal things that girls of her age did. So I took her along to the guide group at the beginning of this year, and to start with they were very enthusiastic and took a lot of time with her. But as time has gone on, unless I'm with her constantly, she misses out on so much. Also, I think a lot of the activities they do are far too in depth for her to be able to cope with. In gaining badges, for instance, there is a tremendous amount of work involved for Joanne, in hours spent both for her and for me. I really wonder what the purpose is because there is nothing at the end of it for her except a badge. She works very hard at school and then to go out to what should be an enjoyable evening at guides only to find she is given more work to do.

The ideal would be to have a special guide group attached to the special school she attends, because that would be a central point. There are a lot of deaf children of her age in the area, so to me that would seem the best solution. She would be able to get the benefit of the guide group but the badges would be changed to suit their particular handicap.

They would still have to work for their badges, but in a different way.

Just occasionally it occurs to me that Joanne will never hear my voice or hear the things that I enjoy, the birds and the wind or water, and I get depressed about that. But I don't allow myself to wallow in depression. I try and think about something positive instead, otherwise I think I could sink a bit lower if I allowed myself to do that. It does happen occasionally; I think it always will.

Regarding my relationship with my husband, I think it has drawn us really close together. We have a common aim with Joanne to educate her to the best of our ability; it has extended our own horizons tremendously. We have become involved in all sorts of things that we wouldn't normally have thought about. We have become involved together. Any little battle we have, we sort out together. As to the effects on my other two children, I don't really know. They are both very patient and quiet and caring to Joanne, but maybe they would have been anyway. They would have been quiet people, I think it's their nature. But on the other hand perhaps it has taught them to appreciate handicapped people's problems more.

Having Joanne has certainly broadened my life considerably. I have become involved in groups and things that I would never have had anything to do with at all, and met far more people. I have developed assertion which I probably wouldn't have to the same degree, because I have had to fight for her in all sorts of ways. We have had to compromise a little – perhaps we would have lived out of the city if we hadn't had to stay near a special school for Joanne. But really, I consider I have made the best out of that situation and adjusted accordingly. Other than that I don't really think I have changed. Perhaps I might have worked a bit more, longer hours in my profession, perhaps have been more involved in that whereas I work part-time and I like it that way at present.

At the moment I'm concerned about Joanne's schooling, she has had a carrot dangled in front of her, in that she has been told that next year, if she's a good girl and works hard, she can go into a hearing class, which I think is wrong. I don't think it's fair on a teacher, or on the other children or on the deaf child, to put her in that situation, without a really effective back-up. We haven't been consulted about this at all. So when

I suggested to Joanne that she will always be in a unit because that is the best for her she told me that this is wrong and that she should be aiming towards a hearing world, which is impossible. So my husband and I will have to do something about this, sort it out with the headmaster at the special school, which we will do shortly. These problems occur every now and then. There has been a lack of communication; certainly there was no meeting with the parents to discuss her future. I think it was very wrong to do this to a child who is handicapped. To give them something to look forward to which is not going to be.

Another concern is for the future. As Joanne is 12 years old it won't be very long before she leaves school. The job situation isn't good at the moment; I can't see that it will improve greatly by then. She is a very intelligent child and will need a stimulating job and it is a concern as to what will be available to her. Will she need further education to get the sort of stimulating job she needs? I would be prepared to work very hard to get her further education if she needs it, either in this country or overseas.

Regarding professionals working in the field, I'd like them to listen to parents, to really listen to what parents are saying. Parents have a lot to offer and they have the child 24 hours a day. I think that what they say is quite valid. I think professionals should take it into consideration more. They must try to understand what the parent is saying and take time with them. I suppose that is hard in a busy world but I think that it is very important. They must treat people as individuals.

I think parents have a right to live their own lives and have interests of their own. It is a very demanding life having a handicapped child and you do tend to become very involved with that child or with groups to do with the handicap. Particularly the mother needs to have her own interests and not feel guilty about it. She needs to get completely away and think about something else for some of the time. The whole family has to be considered. It is very easy to live your life around the handicapped child, whereas everybody in the family has their own personality that has to be developed and their own interests. So it has to be balanced. I think you need a sense of humour. Above anything, if you can keep a sense of humour I think you can make it.

### 3.3 ACCOUNT BY A FATHER OF A 5-YEAR-OLD GIRL WITH DOWN'S SYNDROME

We have been married eight years and we had Sally in our third year of marriage. She is now almost 6 and has Down's syndrome, Trisomy 21, the most common sort of Down's syndrome. We also have Anthony who is about 2½ and is normal apart from a few eyesight problems and Rachel who is now 2½ months.

When Sally was born all my in-laws said she was a lovely child and I thought everything in the garden was lovely. But two days later my wife rang me up at school. I was teaching. The headmaster came storming in and said 'There's something wrong, your wife's in tears, come to the phone.' So I dropped everything, while he looked after my class, and rushed to the phone. I found it very hard to understand what my wife was saying. She was muttering and mumbling things about mongolism, which I really had very little idea about. I had a suspicion that what she was talking about was quite dramatic, so I immediately dropped everything and tore off to the hospital. My wife was very distraught. She was in a room with other mothers. They were unable to understand or cope with the situation. She was immediately moved into another room and I then had to go and see the specialist to find out what it was all about. I didn't know quite how to take the man. He was very direct and perhaps a bit morbid as well. At that stage Sally was under fluorescent lights as she had very bad jaundice. He suggested that it was quite likely she would die. Then he started to explain what Down's syndrome was, and that these children would obtain a mental age of 8, if they survive. That now many of them do survive but a lot of them die before the age of 30 and, that it was quite likely that she would die at an early age. He then proceeded to tell me all the details of her condition.

At the time I was very confused and worried about my wife's condition. She was under a lot of stress. I was initially a little bit angry. Why should this happen to me, or to us? I did a lot of crying, mostly in private. My wife had to stay in hospital and I went back to the flat. My in-laws were very good to me. It took about a couple of days before I could even believe it. I think then I was angry. I was a little bit angry about the way

I was told. I think it could have been done much more compassionately than by telling me all in one breath that not only was my daughter handicapped, but she was likely to die, with the implication that I would be lucky if she did. At that stage I was hoping that she would.

So initially I was told on my own. The paediatrician saw my wife and myself about two weeks after the birth. I think that rather than being told clinically, in a very strange environment, we should have been told together, where we could have supported each other. The other thing that is very important is that you should be told gradually rather than being told all the gory details at the outset. I think professionals who inform parents of such things should be trained in counselling. They need to be aware of how the message is being received because I think that quite often a lot of what is said is only half heard or interpreted the way the parent is able to see it at that particular time, and a lot of information is lost in the conversation. They should have up-to-date information. The paediatrician who gave us the diagnosis said that the information he had on Down's syndrome was at least 15 to 20 years out of date. Also, he tended to highlight the negative aspects of the condition, and very few of the positive aspects were mentioned.

The hospital sister gave us a book to read which my wife couldn't read at the time but I read and found very helpful. But that was sort of *ad hoc*. I think it would have been helpful if somebody who had actually been through it before could have been available to speak to us, really as a model of what to expect in the years to come. At that stage your future horizons had been lowered considerably and you live from day to day. Every day becomes a problem, a hassle, and I think if you can see a bit further ahead it helps.

I've already mentioned that my wife was rather distraught at first. She was almost unintelligible for a while. Fits of sobbing, depression, just completely overcome by the situation. It took a month before any sort of regular behaviour pattern, that I was accustomed to, appeared. I suppose part of the reason was my reaction to it. My parents were very strange. I told my mother first. It was as much as I could do to tell her. Sally was the first grandchild on both sides and my father had already mentioned, on seeing her the first day, words to the effect that 'She'll be a cracker at 18'. That sort of stuck in my mind when I had to tell my mother and father. I don't know why it stuck in my mind but it did. My mother, being a very panicky person said 'Oh, is the baby all right?'. It's the first time I have ever seen my father cry in public. He was absolutely shattered. He didn't know what to do.

My wife's parents are very humanitarian people. They were very concerned. Her mother is a teacher. They were actually told first apart from ourselves and they were very supportive. I don't think they really knew what to do but they were just there if we needed them.

I'm an only child, but my wife has a brother. On the first day he had said to his mother that the baby could be mongoloid. We actually heard this later. My wife and her brother are not particularly close, they irritate each other a lot. They are much closer now than they were, I think. It had the effect of drawing them together slightly.

I didn't want to see my friends. We became very isolated as a result of it. We drifted away from a lot of the friends we had. We have come back to two or three of them that we had originally but our friends seem to have changed. I found that I couldn't talk to friends. I couldn't face them. My wife was in the same situation and we drifted away from a lot of the friends we had made. I think this is a little bit sad in the sense that I was very close to quite a few guys who had played soccer with me since I was very young. We were very close, having played in the same team. We knew each other's weaknesses and strengths and we socialized together. After Sally was born they just completely faded out of existence. One or two of them made contact but it was usually by telephone. I always found an excuse to opt out of anything, and they didn't push it. I suppose knowing the situation they just didn't push it, and we drifted apart. On hindsight, perhaps if we had made the effort to adjust and be able to face them I think perhaps we could have still continued the friendships. I actually gave up soccer after that and a lot of the social contacts I had.

The most helpful support we have had has come from family members. If our immediate family had opted out of the situation, I think we would have been in a worse situation than has actually turned out. My wife's parents especially were very, almost over-helpful. I think my parents took longer to adjust, but have since come round and they are quite a good source of support now. Professionals – well there was a lack of support in the sense that any professional contact we had, had to be initiated by us rather than the other way round. That's not saying that we would have accepted some professional help if it had been offered.

We had a very good family doctor. He actually retired about a year after Sally was born and that was another hurdle we had to overcome. But this particular guy was very well trained. He let us talk to him about it, bounce back ideas and sorts of things we could do. When he left the scene, we went through six or seven different doctors until we found one that we felt comfortable with. I remember a particular incident well. Sally, being Down's syndrome, is very prone to colds and respiratory ailments, in fact she has a runny nose almost indefinitely and it has been so right through. She was hospitalized twice every year for the first three or four years of her life. On one particular occasion Sally was on a down-turn, she was getting worse and her temperature was going up. We went to a doctor and were told that she was teething, and he gave her some antibiotics, standard antibiotics. That afternoon, a friend of ours who happens to be a nurse came round and said that our daughter should be in hospital. She was just lying on the floor and wouldn't move. Within two or three hours she was on a drip in intensive care! So we were not very happy with the help we got from that doctor.

Parent support wasn't available to us at that particular time. If it was we weren't aware of it. We came into contact virtually by bumping into people through agencies that we had to go to. We became involved with the local branch of the Society for the Mentally Handicapped sometime in the second year. We initiated that. It wasn't even mentioned to us before that stage. People, acquaintances, actually said 'Oh I know a lady who's got a daughter with Down's syndrome. Would you like to have a talk with her? Would you like to meet them?' We actually went around to see these particular people. They had a Down's syndrome son. He was at the stage of learning to say simple words, in the pre-reading stage, and we were most impressed by their very enthusiastic way of trying to help this child. At this time of course, Sally was very much a baby. She was only at the stage of rolling over, everything was very slow.

The local early intervention team was brilliant. I'm not sure when they entered the scene, but they came in at a fairly early stage. I think it was the first six months. Of all the professionals, they were the best, as far as help, exercises and various toning up things that Sally had to go through. I think they initiated putting us on to other parents who had Down's syndrome children. It was through this contact that we formed an association of Down's syndrome parents. We got together and decided that we were perhaps a little disillusioned with the Society for the Mentally Handicapped. That they were rather big and bureaucratic and that they weren't giving us the sort of support we wanted. We decided to form a Down's Association. I wasn't on the original committee but I was on pretty soon afterwards. I think the Down's Association was something we got involved with after we came to terms with our situation – although I think that is a bad expression as I don't think we have come to terms with it totally, after we had adjusted anyway, to part of the situation we were in. We found that the group was very self-supportive. We had barbecues and social contact. We have since developed many friends through it. When we look at our friends, they've just about all got something wrong in their families. There are still other friends that we have, from teaching and other areas of life, but a lot of our friends just happen to have Down's syndrome children. The Association is a very mutually supporting group, we don't really get into a lot of contact about trouble shooting or problem solving, we're more social, although a lot of people within the Down's Association have formed little groups of twos and threes who ring each other up and talk to each other.

I've got a close friend whose children I've actually taught, who happened to be the nurse who visited us at home for the first year after Sally was born. I'm pretty sure if she had the information available she would have put us on to it but I'm not sure if she did. I think in the main we actually approached people when we found out what professionals and support services were available. So it really came from us. I don't know whether it was because they weren't sure we were ready or whether they were just waiting for us to make the first move.

There seems to be a lack of structure, if you like, a lack of training on behalf of the agencies that are available to Down's syndrome children. It's very likely that a lot of children with Down's syndrome slip through the net completely. We found that the information on Down's syndrome as a condition, was very sparse. The Down's Association here have recently written a booklet for parents. We borrowed the layout from an Australian magazine which is intended to help parents of new Down's syndrome children and re-wrote it to suit our situation. That was made available so that if parents do have a Down's syndrome child, they can have information available to them.

It is hard to say whether we have totally accepted the situation after five years or whether we are still going through some sort of adjustment. I think we are adjusting all the time. I think our perceptions are changing. I think you go through stages but I don't know whether it is continual or whether you flashback. I find I go through stages where I'm very depressed and I sort of look at my child and say 'What's going to happen in the future?' and I feel very, very sorry for myself. You sort of go up hill and then you slip back. You're gradually trying to achieve the pinnacle but I don't know whether you can say you've adjusted. You have obviously accepted it but you're not necessarily finished adjusting to it. For example, I'm a teacher and I'm looking at other children all the time and occasionally I'd look at one and say 'Oh why couldn't Sally be like that' or 'What's going to happen to Sally?' That sort of thing. How am I going to educate her, deal with toilet training and all the other sorts of little stages that children go through, which with Down's are so much delayed.

Also, Sally has just been through the psychological barrier if you like, of the 5-year-old test for school placement. She's been at a pre-school centre since she was about two and she's done reasonably well there. I think now she's sort of got to the stage where she's grown out of it, she's 5 and she's still there. At this stage we'll leave her there until she's 6. We've had her tested on the Stanford–Binet which is a language-based test. That is Sally's biggest failure – language. It's her weakest area and of course she scored around an IQ of 45-50 which is very low. But really her mental age is less than 3 years so it's what could be expected. Actually, my wife had more trouble than me adjusting to this. The fact that she had such a poor IQ and future prospects were so bad that I think we went through the grieving process again. Anger comes into it quite a lot. I don't slam doors exactly, but I sort of grit my teeth and hammer walls occasionally as an outlet. I found that after this particular incident it took me quite a while to come to terms. I don't know if I've come to terms with it now, we still have the same problem of having to find somewhere for Sally to go.

Without a doubt having Sally has drawn my wife and I much closer together. We have been told that a handicapped child can also have the opposite effect, where perhaps the husband or the wife can't cope and decide to opt out of the situation rather than face it. For some reason we decided to fight and try and overcome it together and I think that our relationship has benefited from that. We are communicating better, getting at feelings rather than mundane sorts of things such as finances and things like that. We're much more able to talk about issues that come up. It would be nice to think that we didn't have to go through that to get better communication and it would have been interesting to know how we would have got on had Sally been a normal child, whether it would have had the same effect.

The other children, of course, came along after. I think the position in the family of the handicapped child is very critical. With Sally we had to, and we still are, fighting all the way for provision for education for just her general development, her language, her reading, the things that matter for her coping in society. We put a lot of work into it. When we had Anthony, our second, he benefited because a lot of the things we did with Sally we did automatically with Anthony. We are teachers, both of us, so we do have some insight into development. With Anthony, I don't know whether it's because of the input we've given him or whether he was like that at birth, but he's quite advanced for his age, not only physically but intellectually as well.

Sally has had a negative effect on Anthony in that children do learn by modelling. Sally sometimes talks gibberish, and has fits of frustration which develop into rage when she can't communicate. Also, she often finds it hard to communicate what she wants and when nobody can understand her she begins stamping her feet and lying on the floor. Anthony has inherited some of these things although he's overcoming that somewhat now. I think, also, by virtue of the fact that he's got a handicapped sister, he's had to adjust to her in the sense that, although she is older than him, he is now the major sibling, if you like. They were at the same stage for quite a while. He's miles past her in language now. He actually looks after Sally. It's nice to see but I think it's a bit of a burden on a 2½ year old.

Because Sally is handicapped we have had to put a lot of work into her as far as extra attention and structured materials go. My wife's mother was a primary school teacher and she is a very good teacher. She's spent a lot of time with Sally, one to one, on matching and that sort of thing. When Anthony appeared on the scene, we were aware that Sally was demanding a lot of our attention and we were concerned about Anthony and his situation. I think that now in some ways we've adjusted to the fact that Sally is not our only child and that we have to make allowances for the others.

Having Sally has changed the whole direction of my life. I was very much a sporty person. I still am to some extent but not to the same degree. I think that having a handicapped child made me more family orientated, although I could have become that anyway through having children. Also, since I've had Sally I've been involved with the Down's Association committee. I have been on the local executive committee of the Society for the Mentally Handicapped and I've been through a parent-to-parent support training course, all of which would not have happened if I had not had Sally. Also, after what we went through, we feel we've got something to offer parents who are about to go through it, or are in the stages of going through it.

From what people have told me I have undergone a personality change in the sense that I've become more confident, I think through having to fight to get things done for Sally such as regarding her constant eye and ear infections which has meant considerable contact with professionals. We've had to put our point of view fairly succinctly and try and be forceful. I've become far more confident in the oral sense. I also believe that I am more tolerant. Teaching shouldn't really have been something I got into. I used to be very impatient, and also intolerant of anybody else who didn't toe the line. My teaching style was very disciplinarian. I am now much more democratic with children. In fact I went through a stage where I was completely child orientated, rather than being teacher orientated but I've now come back and tried to balance it up.

At the present time we have quite a few concerns about Sally. The one we've come to at the moment is her placement in an educational institution after she leaves the pre-school centre. We're resolved to her staying there until she's 6. She's now 5½. We also are aware that the likely places she could go are very full and that there are a lack of facilities, in our particular area, which can supply the sort of education that we want. The options that are available are rather limited. There are special classes within normal schools but a lot of those have children who are not necessarily mentally handicapped. They can be socially maladjusted, and that's affected their learning. Therefore, some of the behaviour of those children is less than desirable. Since Down's children learn by modelling, if they are exposed to any deviant models that's the sort of behaviour they are going to exhibit. Another alternative is that there are satellite classes of special schools placed in regular schools, the aim of which is to make the mentally handicapped more suitable for a 'normal' classroom situation. Then there are special schools.

All these particular ways of trying to educate Sally are not particularly suitable because of the modelling aspect. She will model on any behaviour that is around her and she has proven this time and time again. Ideally, we would like her to be in a normal school, perferably in a small class with some support from special education, where people are trained in handling mentally handicapped children, that is, some special education input, but preferably with an ordinary teacher. The problem of course is not making a burden on that teacher so that Sally becomes the focal point of the classroom. It has got to be a balance, but where she can take part in the normal sort of things that kids do in a school, knowing how to behave, when to be quiet, when to talk, things that make people socially acceptable.

Having a child with Down's syndrome has also affected my career. I'm a teacher and so is my wife. When we were first married before we had Sally, the best way to get ahead in teaching was to become your own boss as soon as possible, so we applied for two teacher schools in all corners of the country. We tried everything but we didn't succeed. We then decided to have children and along came Sally. Since we've had Sally, my wife has wanted to be very close to her mother because she gets a lot of support from her. This has really meant that I was restricted to applying for jobs in the same city in which we live, where she could have contact with her mother. I don't know whether it is true, but I still believed the way to get promotion at that particular age was to try and move about. So I applied for literally thousands of jobs after having Sally, in this area and had almost given up hope when along came a senior teacher's job at a local school. I've been here now five years and we've had a constant conflict about me always wanting to move again to get promotion. I also had an urge to see the country through teaching as well. This is my personal aim if you like, but of course having Sally virtually immobilized us in this area.

Our aim for Sally's future is very clear, we want her to be as self-sufficient as possible. The current trends indicate that while she'll be pretty good on self-care, she will not be able to provide for herself in the sense of monetary support or any career, or that sort of thing. She'll always be dependent on us, or some agency. We obviously love Sally and are concerned about her condition and want to do the best by her. Our aim really at this stage is to build a flat attached to our house where she can have her own front door and we would be there if she needs us. Even that might be a little bit too optimistic, at this stage. Having had Sally, we tend to look ahead one day at a time; well that's not really true, we tend to look at things in very short time frames, so we have achievable goals. So the long term future is really not our concern at this stage.

We feel the key is to live one day at a time. Because if you don't you will find that you will create too many problems for yourself trying to look ahead. Also, what is a problem now needs to be addressed before you can do anything else. It is good to know also that you're not alone, other people have got similar problems and some a damn sight worse problems than what you've got. My child's got Down's syndrome with a mild heart defect which really doesn't have any effect on her. She's mildly handicapped. If you visit institutions you see kids that can't walk, can't talk, they are almost vegetables and yet the people are coping with them. So you must always keep things in perspective. Things could be better, but they could be a damn sight worse.

I think that you do need support of some kind, whether it is a close friend or a member of your family or somebody else who has been through a similar thing. Also I don't think in the early stages that you are particularly rational and I think that quite often you need to fight with yourself and you need to do things you wouldn't normally do, for your particular child. When you've adjusted you need to be encouraged to think for yourself. You need to be told to fight. So you need professionals who are well trained and can help you. There perhaps should be one who is a co-ordinator, who's sole responsibility is to govern, in consultation with you, what your child should do. I think professionals should have training in interpersonal skills, as well as in their own particular sphere of medicine or psychology, say. They must have the interpersonal skills to go along with it.

## 3.4 CONCLUSIONS

In addition to the fact that the above are moving accounts by these parents of their experiences, many of the issues discussed in the previous chapter were commented on by the parents. While there were notable similarities between the two accounts, there were also interesting differences. One important difference was in the way the parents reacted to the diagnosis of disability. Whereas the mother experienced relief on being told her daughter was deaf, the father and his wife were clearly traumatized by the news that their daughter had Down's syndrome. This difference was probably mainly due to the fact that the mother had suspected that her daughter had a problem for several months and therefore had done some grieving already. Also, she was probably relieved to be told that the problem was deafness and as she viewed it, 'not anything more serious'. It is also likely that the trauma experienced by the second set of parents was accentuated by the way they were told about the disability by a professional who was apparently insensitive, out of date, and did not tell the parents together or follow the other guidelines on communicating diagnoses which were discussed in Chapter 2.

While the way he was given the diagnosis was a bone of contention for the father, the mother's complaint was about how long it took to get her suspicions confirmed that her daughter was deaf. That two professionals were not willing to take her observations seriously and that she was referred to the audiologist only 'to keep her happy' is a matter of concern. Such stories are heard far too frequently from parents for them to be dismissed lightly, particularly but not exclusively those with deaf children. Not only is it bad for parents' self-esteem to be treated in this way, but also, vital time is lost for providing appropriate training in order to facilitate the children's development.

Another difference between the accounts is that the father's family received a lot of help and support from their extended family members, particularly the grandparents, whereas the mother reported that she had received no help at all from her extended family. The fact that the father commented on how vital this help was highlights the difficulties experienced by parents who do not get such support. This reinforces the point that professionals should not assume that parents will receive help from extended family and therefore should make sure that parents are helped to identify and access other possible sources of support.

It is interesting that both parents commented on their difficulties in accessing appropriate services and support groups. In both cases some of the help the parents valued most, which ought to have come about through professional referral or suggestions, actually came to them via chance meetings with other people. This is a haphazard situation which would not happen if professionals were fulfilling their information function with parents, but it is fairly typical in my experience.

Another similarity which emerged from the accounts was the sense of isolation felt by both parents and how much they valued contacts with other parents of children with disabilities. Yet again, these contacts were generally made by chance, they had not been instigated by the professionals involved.

Both parents commented on how having a child with a disability had brought them and their spouse closer together and had also made them more confident and assertive through having to battle for services. Both parents considered that their careers had been affected. For the father there had been both positive and negative effects, for the mother it was seen as mainly negative. Also, both parents commented on their awareness of possible negative effects on their other children and discussed how they attempted to compensate for these.

An important factor that emerged from both accounts was the key role that the family doctor played in their lives. Having a knowledgeable and supportive family doctor was seen as essential by both parents. Not having an effective collaborative relationship with their doctor was clearly a major source of stress for these families.

Finally, both parents commented on the need for professionals to improve their listening and interpersonal skills. Listening to parents is one of the four aspects of professional helping noted in Chapter 1, and is also the subject of Chapter 5.

It is realized, of course, that the two accounts presented in this chapter are simply the views of two parents. The similarities and differences in these accounts reinforce the need for professionals to understand the likely reactions of parents and the possible effects on family life without assuming that these will always apply. Since every parent, and every family, will react to and cope with a child with a disability in a different way, professionals must be prepared to treat all parents as individuals and plan their interventions to take into account parents' idiosyncratic needs and strengths.

## 3.5 SUMMARY

In order to get parents' perspectives of the effects of their children with disabilities on themselves and their families two parents were interviewed and their accounts presented in this chapter. The parents interviewed were the mother of a 12-year-old girl with profound hearing impairment and the father of a 5-year-old girl with Down's syndrome. There were interesting similarities and differences in the two accounts and many of the issues discussed in the previous chapter were commented on by the parents.

Both parents discussed at length their interactions with professionals. One conclusion which can be drawn from their comments is that some general guidelines for professional collaboration with parents are needed. This is the subject of the next chapter.

# 4

# Model for working
# with parents

## 4.1 INTRODUCTION

In the first two chapters of this book it was argued that developing collaborative relationships with parents is essential if professionals are to be effective in working with children with disabilities. The two accounts by parents of their experiences of caring for their children (with hearing impairment and mental handicap) support the importance of parent–professional partnerships but also demonstrate that relationships between parents and professionals are often problematic. In this chapter specific suggestions regarding how parents and professionals should relate to one another are considered and a theoretical model which provides guidelines for the practice of parent involvement is presented.

In Chapter 2, the specialist knowledge regarding families of children with disabilities which professionals need in order to work effectively with them was discussed in depth. However, this knowledge alone will not be sufficient for professionals to be able to develop collaborative relationships with parents. Also needed are certain facilitative attitudes on behalf of both professionals and parents. Lehr and Lehr (1990) have made separate lists of the required attitudes in the form of recommendations to professionals and parents. These lists are presented below.

### 4.1.1 Recommendations to professionals

- Always treat individuals with disabilities and their families with respect;
- Take account of cultural, ethnic and racial practices in planning treatment;
- Be clear about the principles and values that underpin your treatment programmes;
- Use language and terminology that family members can understand;
- Be honest with parents about what you and your agency can and cannot do;
- Be open to learning from parents and individuals with disabilities;
- Establish working relationships with family members based on mutual respect;
- Respect privacy and confidentiality;
- Don't stereotype families with disabled members, get to know them as individuals;
- Don't assign blame to parents or say anything which could make them feel guilty;
- Be willing to admit you make mistakes.

### 4.1.2 Recommendations to parents

- Always treat professionals with respect;
- Educate others about your cultural, racial or ethnic beliefs and practices;
- Remember that professionals are not miracle workers who can meet all your needs;
- Be honest about your capabilities and limitations;
- Know what you value and what you want;
- Know where you are willing to compromise;
- Share information with professionals to assist them in meeting your needs;
- Be willing to learn from professionals;
- Be willing to admit you make mistakes.

These attitudes on the part of parents and professionals provide a basis for meaningful collaboration between the two. The possible forms which that collaboration can take are discussed in the following section which presents a theoretical model for providing guidance to professionals regarding the establishment of parent–professional partnerships.

## 4.2 RATIONALE FOR THE MODEL

In the past fifteen years a great deal has been written about how professionals can be of help to parents of children with disabilities (Gargiulo, 1985; Seligman, 1991; Stewart, 1986). There is now a substantial amount of information on this subject including discussion of a wide range of strategies available to practitioners for working with parents. What has so far been missing from this literature is a comprehensive, theoretical model to provide guidelines for professional practice with parents. A theoretical model would provide professionals with a framework with which to formulate overall policy and plans for their involvement with parents. Such a model would enable each organization to ensure that, as far as possible, parents' needs are being met and their potential contributions are being utilized.

The model for working with parents presented in this chapter was developed by the author (Hornby, 1989) and adapted with help from a colleague, Ray Murray, in New Zealand. It has been validated by numerous groups of parents and professionals and has been used to train groups of professionals in the skills required for working with parents in England, New Zealand and India (Hornby, 1990; Hornby and Peshawaria, 1991). The proposed model for working with parents is presented in Fig. 4.1.

## 4.3 MODEL FOR WORKING WITH PARENTS

The model consists of two pyramids, one representing a hierarchy of parents' needs, the other a hierarchy of parents' potential contributions. The pyramids are intended to demonstrate visually the different levels of needs and contributions of parents. That is, it is meant to show that, while all parents have some needs and some potential contributions a smaller number have an intense need for guidance, or the capability of making extensive contributions. For example, whereas all parents need to have good communication with

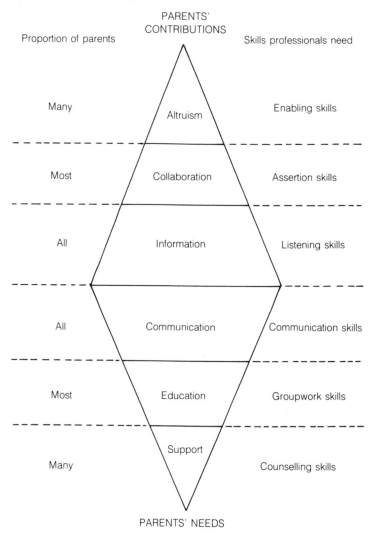

**Figure 4.1** Model for working with parents.

professionals a much smaller number will need supportive counselling at any point in time.

Built into the model is the idea that different professional skills are needed for each level of the two pyramids. It should also be noted that more time and expertise is generally required by professionals in order to work at higher levels of the pyramids. For example, providing supportive counselling to parents takes more time and demands a higher level of professional expertise than establishing good communication with parents.

Each of the components of the model will now be explained and the knowledge and skills needed by professionals in order to fulfil each function with parents will be identified. The areas in which parents can contribute are discussed first, followed by parents' needs.

### 4.3.1 Information

All parents can contribute valuable information about their children with disabilities. Information concerning childrens' likes and dislikes, strengths and weaknesses, along with any relevant medical details can be gathered by professionals at face-to-face meetings or by telephone. Many parents feel more comfortable on their own territory and generally appreciate it when professionals offer to visit them there. A home visit can also be useful for meeting other members of the family and for gaining an understanding of the situation parents are coping with at home. Gaining an impression of the home circumstances and making full use of parents' knowledge of their children leads to more effective professional practice. In addition, it makes parents feel that they have been listened to and that an active interest has been taken in their children. In order to fulfil these functions professionals need to develop good listening skills. These are discussed in Chapter 5.

### 4.3.2 Collaboration

Most parents are willing and able to contribute more than just information. Most parents are able to collaborate with professionals by following up treatment programmes at home. This could be something as simple as administering medication or may be carrying out exercises suggested by the speech therapist or physiotherapist, or behaviour management programmes suggested by the psychologist.

However, some parents, at some times, are not willing to do this. It may be that their resources are already fully committed in coping with their children at home, so they are not able to do anything extra. This is one situation when making home visits can be useful in allowing professionals to see exactly what parents have to cope with. Often professional resentment at parents' apparent lack of co-operation can turn into admiration for their ability to cope with seemingly impossible conditions. At a later time family circumstances may change and parents may then want to become more involved in treatment programmes with their children. Therefore, professionals must respect parents' rights to make this decision on behalf of their children with disabilities and be prepared to accept that although they must offer all parents the opportunity to collaborate with them, some parents will not take this up until possibly some time in the future.

However, since most parents do wish to collaborate, and it is almost always to their children's advantage, professionals should make a point of attempting to involve all parents in their children's treatment programmes. For parents who are reluctant to participate professionals need to be able to assertively put the case for them being involved without pressuring parents into taking on extra work for which they don't have the time or the energy. For those parents who agree to participate but then don't follow through, professionals need to sensitively check the reasons for this and then attempt to problem-solve any difficulties and work with parents on finding solutions to these. Therefore, professionals need the skills of collaborating with parents in a flexible working partnership. This involves the use of the listening skills noted above but also the use of assertion skills which are discussed in Chapter 7.

### 4.3.3 Altruism

Many parents, after having come to terms with their child's disability, and having established some stability in their family lives, begin to feel altruistic, particularly towards other parents with disabled children. Many of these parents have both the time and the ability to help others in various ways. Some may wish to act as voluntary aides, either assisting in work with children, or in the preparation of materials. Some parents are able to contribute their expertise through membership of parent or professional organizations. Others may wish to get involved in setting up or helping with a parent support or advocacy group. Still others may be able to provide emotional and practical support to other parents, for example, through parent-to-parent schemes (Chapter 8). Some parents will have the confidence and ability to provide in-service training for professionals by speaking at conferences or workshops, or by writing about their experiences.

Professionals should continually be on the look-out for parents who can contribute in this way, so that their assets can be used to the full. In these times of contracting resources professionals should make sure that they make optimum use of this valuable voluntary resource. In order to do this they need the listening and assertion skills noted above, plus the skills of enabling which are discussed in Chapter 9.

### 4.3.4 Communication

All parents of children with disabilities need to have effective channels of communication with the professionals who work with their children. They need information about the services professionals can provide and they need to understand their rights and responsibilities. Parents also look to professionals for feedback on how their children are doing. Parents need to feel that they can contact the professionals directly when they have a concern about their child. They typically regard professionals as a major source of information and support and therefore need to have a working partnership with them. Professionals can facilitate this by establishing a variety of forms of contact with parents such as through telephone calls and home visits in addition to meeting parents at their office or clinic. Therefore, professionals need to develop effective communication skills, including the listening and assertion skills discussed in Chapters 5 and 7.

### 4.3.5 Education

Most parents are keen to obtain guidance from professionals which is aimed at promoting their children's progress or managing their behaviour. Some parents would rather receive such guidance on an individual basis while others are interested in participating in group parent education programmes of one kind or another. These programmes are often referred to as parent workshops. The most effective format of parent workshops seems to be one which combines educational input with opportunities for parents to share concerns and ideas. Such workshops are discussed in Chapter 8. In order to effectively provide guidance to parents professionals need to have good listening and assertion skills, as discussed in Chapters 5 and 7. In order to conduct parent workshops professionals also need to develop the skills of group facilitation, which are discussed in Chapter 8.

### 4.3.6 Support

Many parents of children with disabilities will, at one time or another, be in need of supportive counselling. Although some parents cope extremely well with the demands of raising children with disabilities without ever needing such counselling others definitely benefit greatly from it. Supportive counselling should therefore be made available to all parents from diagnosis of the disability onwards, even though a large proportion of parents may seldom need it. Typically, parents will approach the professionals who work with their children, rather than professional counsellors, in search of help for the problems which concern them. Professionals should therefore have a level of basic counselling skills sufficient to be good listeners and to help parents solve everyday problems. They should also have the skills and knowledge to be able to refer parents on to professional counsellors when problems raised are beyond their level of competence. In order to address these requirements, counselling skills and a three-stage problem-solving model of counselling are discussed in Chapter 6.

### 4.4 CONCLUSION

Using the model for working with parents described here, a comprehensive policy for parent involvement can be developed to suit each professional setting. The model can be used for guidance in ensuring that procedures are in place to meet the needs of parents and to check that their potential contributions are being fully utilized. In addition, the model suggests that, for parent involvement policies to be successfully implemented, professionals must develop certain interpersonal skills. It suggests that listening, assertion, counselling, group work and enabling skills are required by professionals in order to work effectively with parents of children with disabilities. The development and use of these skills is considered in the remaining chapters of this book.

### 4.5 SUMMARY

Although the necessity for professionals to develop productive working relationships with parents is widely agreed, in practice this does not always occur. It is argued that the adoption of certain facilitative attitudes by both professionals and parents is necessary. A theoretical model for working with parents is also necessary in order to provide guidance to professionals in meeting parents' needs and making use of their potential contributions. The model presented in this chapter describes parents' contributions in terms of information, collaboration and altruism and parents' needs in terms of communication, education and support. In order to implement the requirements of the model professionals need to develop certain interpersonal skills. These skills are elaborated in the remainder of this book. In the following chapter the listening skills needed by professionals are discussed.

# 5

---

# Listening skills

## 5.1 IMPORTANCE OF LISTENING

Whenever I have discussed parent–professional relationships with groups of parents who have children with disabilities one area has unfailingly emerged as the focus of greatest dissatisfaction. This is the poor quality and limited amount of listening which professionals engage in when interacting with parents. From the parents' perspective professionals do too much talking and too little listening. This leaves some parents feeling that there is a lot which they would have liked to have communicated to the professionals. Other parents infer that professionals are not able or not willing to listen to their concerns.

Listening is a vitally important skill for both our work and personal lives. It is something that most people think they have no difficulty with but, in my experience, the vast majority of people are poor listeners. The reason for this confusion is that hearing is often mistaken for listening. In order to clarify the distinction between these two skills several writers (Gargiulo, 1985; Kroth, 1985) have described four categories which distinguish hearing from listening, taking into account whether the person is actively or passively engaged in the activity. The categories are: passive hearing; active hearing; passive listening; and active listening.

### 5.1.1 Passive hearing

This is the skill in which we hear what someone is saying while paying minimal attention to it, so that when we are accused of not listening we can deny this by repeating their actual words. However, this is seldom found to be satisfactory since the person talking is attempting to get a message across, not to have someone parrot their words. So passive hearing is of little use except when one wants to irritate one's spouse, at which times it is a guaranteed success!

### 5.1.2 Active hearing

This is often used in everyday conversation and involves hearing what people say sufficiently so that a word or phrase they have used provides an opportunity for us to enter the conversation with our own comments. It is the skill needed to survive social situations in which one is expected to make polite conversation and is most skilfully employed by people who like to constantly steer the conversation around to themselves. It is clear then that with active hearing people are attempting to meet their own needs rather than pay attention to those of others.

### 5.1.3 Passive listening

This occurs when complete attention is given to the person being listened to. Listeners demonstrate through their non-verbal behaviour that they are fully with the person who is talking. They do not say anything which could act as a block to communication and in fact mainly remain silent. This skill gives people the space to explore their thoughts in a situation where they feel supported. It is therefore extremely useful and is sometimes sufficient to meet the needs of people seeking help.

### 5.1.4  Active listening

This involves the listener being actively engaged in clarifying the thoughts and feelings of the person they are with. It builds on passive listening but goes beyond it in that the main points of what is said are reflected back to the person. This is done to provide a kind of 'sounding board' to facilitate exploration and clarification of the person's concerns and ideas. It is therefore the most useful form of listening when someone has a problem for which they are seeking help.

Active listening is probably the key to competence in interpersonal communication. For example, it is useful in gaining information in an interview situation, in facilitating thoughts and feelings in a counselling context, and in setting up the conditions for conflict resolution when being assertive. Therefore, an important goal of this chapter is to encourage and assist readers to improve their active listening skills.

## 5.2  ATTITUDES REQUIRED FOR EFFECTIVE LISTENING

There are certain key attitudes which are required for effective listening to take place. First of all, there must be a strong desire to understand the other person and to communicate meaningfully with him or her. Second, the listener must have confidence in people's ability to solve their own problems. Third, they must believe in the potency of listening in facilitating this process. Also necessary are the three attitudinal qualities (noted in Chapter 1) which Rogers (1980) described as the core conditions for effective helping relationships: genuineness, respect, and empathy.

### 5.2.1  Genuineness

By genuineness is meant a lack of superficiality. That is, being a real person without the need for a façade or hiding behind a professional role. Rogers also referred to this quality as 'congruence', meaning that the feelings and thoughts experienced were also the ones which were expressed. Bolton (1979) suggests that genuineness has three components: self-awareness; self-acceptance; and self-expression. He argues one needs to be aware of both one's positive and negative thoughts and feelings, to be accepting of these, and to be able to express them, when appropriate, in order to be genuine.

### 5.2.2 Respect

Rogers (1980) also referred to respect as unconditional positive regard, non-possessive love, warmth and acceptance. It involves accepting the right of other people to have their own values which may be quite different from your own. It has been compared with the Greek concept of 'Agape' which refers to a concern for the well being of other people. Bolton (1979) suggests that it is not necessary to like someone in order to show him or her respect. Also, that one need not approve of a person's behaviour in order to be accepting of his or her thoughts and feelings.

### 5.2.3 Empathy

Empathy refers to the ability to see things from another person's perspective, that is, to see the world through someone else's eyes, or as the American Indians put it, 'to walk in another's moccasins'. Rogers (1980) defined it as sensing the other person's feelings as if they were your own, without losing the 'as if' nature of the involvement. It is different from sympathy, which is 'feeling for' someone, in that empathy is 'feeling with' someone. Bolton (1979) explains empathy as having an accurate understanding of the other person's thoughts and feelings while maintaining a separateness from the person. He considers empathy to be the most important quality for enriching interpersonal communication and fostering personal growth.

### 5.3 BLOCKS TO COMMUNICATION

In addition to possessing the above attitudes effective listeners must also avoid certain common barriers or blocks to communication (Bolton, 1979; Gargiulo, 1985; Gordon, 1970). These are ways of interacting with people which we have learnt in order to cope with everyday conversations. Their value is that they keep our involvement on a superficial level, which is generally acceptable when we are not acting in a professional capacity. However, this is not appropriate when we are seeking to be of help to people, so we must be aware of and seek to avoid these blocks to communication, especially when we are attempting to listen to their concerns. The most frequently used blocks are as follows.

### 5.3.1 Reassurance

When we seek to reassure someone by saying, for example, 'Don't worry, I'm sure it'll work out all right', this acts as a block to further communication because the person's view of the situation is given little credence and his or her judgement is belittled. Even if the future could be predicted such false reassurance would still not be helpful since it does not acknowledge or deal with the reality of persons' feelings and perceptions.

### 5.3.2 Denial of feelings

Another barrier to meaningful communication happens when people's feelings are denied or they are told how they should feel. When people are told, 'You shouldn't get so depressed' or it is suggested that they 'cheer up' or 'look on the bright side' this is not helpful and it stifles communication with the person making such statements. For example, one professional's response to a parent of a child with a severe disability who was expressing her concerns and feelings, was to tell her that caring for her child would be 'character building'. Understandably, this comment led to the termination of this meeting and the relationship between the two.

### 5.3.3 False acknowledgement of feelings

A communication block which has the added feature of really annoying someone occurs when people make such statements as, 'I know exactly how you feel'. In addition to the fact that no one can know how another person feels, this kind of statement acts as a barrier to the expression of feelings.

### 5.3.4 Diverting

A strategy commonly used in everyday life when people begin to express strong feelings is to divert them onto another topic. Statements like, 'Let's not dwell on those problems. Tell me about her achievements', serve only to block meaningful communication. Another example of diverting is when humour is used inappropriately to make a joke of a serious concern. Although there are times when humour can be very useful in a helping situation it can seriously backfire when used at the wrong time. Humour can act as a block to communication, fobbing the person off by making a joke of the situation.

### 5.3.5 Advice giving

There are, of course, many situations in which it is appropriate to give advice to people. However, one way of avoiding listening to people's concerns is to immediately give them a piece of advice to deal with the first concern they express. This stops them from exploring their concerns and effectively terminates the interaction, enabling the advice giver to spend the minimum of time in the situation.

When this occurs the effectiveness of professional interactions with parents is significantly reduced. By blocking further communication in this way professionals are only dealing with the first concern raised by parents. The giving of advice stifles the expression of further parental concerns which are likely to be of greater importance than the initial concerns which parents mention. This is because in most helping relationships people tend to mention problems of lesser significance initially in order to see how they are handled. If they feel comfortable about the way these are handled then they will begin to discuss difficulties about which they are more concerned. The giving of advice following expression of the first concern therefore acts as a block to this process and substantially reduces the effectiveness of the help given.

### 5.3.6 Logical argument

One way to block the expression of concerns or feelings is to use logic to argue with the person. This has the effect of focusing on the facts of the situation and avoiding discussing feelings. A common example of this strategy is the use of 'Yes, but . . .'. People who respond to others' concerns or problems with 'Yes, but . . .' are really avoiding dealing with the concern by using logical argument to divert the discussion onto an intellectual level.

### 5.3.7 Inappropriate questioning

There are clearly many times when professionals need to ask questions in their meetings with parents. However, asking too many questions can lead to parents feeling interrogated and therefore act as a barrier to effective communication. Also, some types of questions act as blocks to communication. Foremost of these are questions which deflect parents from exploring their concerns and allow professionals to determine the direction of the conversation. Closed questions which require a yes or no answer are particularly bad in this regard. The type of question most likely to act as a block is the 'Why' question. Asking why someone feels a certain way, or is concerned about something, or did a particular thing, is notoriously unhelpful. Also, since the 'Why' question often carries an implied criticism it is possible for it to be offensive to parents.

### 5.3.8 Criticism

Although professionals may disagree with what parents have done or are doing with their children it is important to realize that criticizing them will act as a block to further communication. Parents may well consider that they are being blamed for creating any problems which they have brought up. It is far better to use techniques such as the DESC script (discussed in Chapter 7) to give feedback to parents and encourage them to change their behaviour.

### 5.3.9 Sarcasm

In order to strengthen a point that is being made it is often tempting to use sarcasm or even ridicule. However, these are high risk strategies since they are certain to block further communication and may be offensive to people.

### 5.3.10 Labelling

Another way to block communication with people is to label them. For example, suggesting to someone that they are 'a worrier' or they are 'a perfectionist' is of little use and will act as a barrier to further communication.

### 5.3.11 Diagnosing

Being over-interpretive about what people are saying, for example, telling them what you think their problem is, will act as a block to further communication. Even if you are right people object to being the subject of amateur psycho-analysis, so your diagnosis is therefore likely to be unhelpful.

### 5.3.12 Moralizing

Telling people what they 'ought to do' or 'should do' or what is the 'right thing' for them to do acts as a block to communication and can be seen as being patronizing. Such moralizing tends to arouse resentment and is seldom helpful.

### 5.3.13 Ordering

When people are told firmly what to do they can become resentful since this implies that they cannot make their own decisions. Ordering people to do such things as carrying out intervention programmes designed by professionals can therefore be counterproductive and block further communication. One needs to be more sensitive in providing guidance to parents.

### 5.3.14 Threatening

Suggesting to people that if they do not carry out certain actions then they will be subject to negative consequences acts as a block to communication. For example, when professionals tell parents that if they don't get their children's behaviour under control now it will be much worse for them later, this detracts from their relationships with parents, even though it may well be true.

### 5.3.15 Inappropriate self-disclosure

Disclosing something about yourself can often be helpful in building productive relationships with other people. However, self-disclosure can also become a block to communication if it focuses the conversation on oneself. We all know people who, when told of a problem someone is having, mention that they have had a similar problem, or they know someone who has, and then go on and on about it. This then becomes a means of fobbing people off by not allowing them to explore their own difficulties.

### 5.3.16 Self-listening

A somewhat different block to communication is created without having to utter a word. While you have been reading the previous section on blocks to communication you are almost certain to have had various thoughts enter into your mind. Some of these thoughts will have been triggered by the content of the section. For example, you may have thought of incidents in your life in which some of the blocks were used. Other thoughts will have been totally unrelated to the contents of the book. For example, you may have thought back to what you were doing earlier in the day or thought ahead to what you will be doing later.

This also occurs during other activities such as watching television, when attending meetings and when listening to someone speak. The phenomenon has been termed 'self-listening' and is thought to be due to the fact that our brain power is not fully utilized when we are processing written or oral communication. Some of the brain's capacity is available for other activities. This is what enables us to read the newspaper or watch television and still hear what our partner has said sufficiently to practise the passive hearing referred to earlier. In fact this skill has other important uses. It enables us to survive excrutiatingly boring meetings and lectures by drifting off into our own thoughts while still maintaining touch with the overall theme of what is going on. However, problems occur when our thoughts become so interesting that we lose track of the activity we are supposed to be engaged in and are asked to comment on what has been said!

This highlights the drawback of self-listening and explains why it is a block to communication. When someone is listening to another person and begins to self-listen there is a likelihood that important aspects of what is said will be missed. The listener may then become confused and will be unable to respond effectively to the other person, who will therefore become aware of the inadequacy of the listening and tend to clam up. This is why it is very important when professionals are listening to parents that they are able to reduce self-listening to a minimum.

Probably the best ways of limiting self-listening are to use the techniques of paraphrasing and active listening which are discussed later in this chapter.

### 5.3.17 Reactions to the blocks

Reading or hearing about the above blocks to communication typically affects people in one or more of the following ways. First, many people recognize that they have been using the blocks in their attempts to help others and feel guilty about the possible damage they have done. Second, some people begin to point out to others when they are using the blocks. This then acts as another block to communication, but is a step along the road toward avoiding using the blocks oneself. Most people, however, feel at a loss as to what they can use instead of the blocks. The answer to this is to use the listening, assertion and counselling skills described in this and the following chapters.

### 5.4 ATTENTIVENESS

In addition to having appropriate attitudes and avoiding blocks to communication, effective listening requires a high level of attentiveness. This involves focusing one's physical attention on the person being listened to, and is often referred to as using attending skills. Egan (1982) considers that there are five major components of attentiveness: maintaining good eye contact; facing the client squarely; leaning toward the other; adopting an open posture; and, remaining relaxed. These components are described below followed by discussion of some additional features of attentiveness.

### 5.4.1 Eye contact

The most important component of attentiveness is main-taining good eye contact. This involves looking directly at the other person's face and only shifting one's gaze to observe any gestures or body movements. Some people find looking directly into another person's eyes uncom-fortable so they should look at the mouth or nose area since the person being listened to will not be able to tell the difference.

In some cultures it is not acceptable for certain members of the society to make eye contact with other members except in certain situations. For example, in many Pacific island countries like Samoa a younger person may not look an elder directly in the eyes. Also, in many Arab countries it is not permitted for women to look into the eyes of men they are not related to. When listening to someone from such cultures one must be sensitive to these constraints and attempt to communicate attentiveness through culturally appropriate means.

Many people in Western societies avoid eye contact when they are talking about their concerns or feelings, either out of embarrassment, or simply so that they can concen-trate on what they are saying. However, the listener should continue to look at the other person's face even when he or she is not looking at them. At some point the person will look at the listener and if there is eye contact will be reassured that he or she is being listened to. So, while it is acceptable for people not to have eye contact when they are speaking it is not recommended when one is acting as a listener.

### 5.4.2 Facing squarely

To communicate attentiveness it is important for the listener to face the other person squarely. Turning one's body away from another person suggests that you are not totally with them. However, some people find that sitting squarely is too intense and can be somewhat intimidating to the other person, so they prefer to sit at a slight angle. This is quite acceptable.

### 5.4.3  Leaning forward

Leaning slightly forward, towards the person being listened to, communicates attentiveness. Alternatively, leaning backwards, worst of all in a slouch, gives the impression that you are not interested in what is being said.

### 5.4.4  Open posture

Having one's legs crossed and, even more so, one's arms crossed when one is listening gives the impression of a lack of openness, as if a barrier is being placed between the listener and the person talking. Attentiveness is communicated by the adoption of an open posture with both arms and legs uncrossed. However, many women feel most comfortable sitting with their legs crossed at the knees and would not be able to remain as relaxed with their legs uncrossed. I have found that this does not significantly reduce their attentiveness.

### 5.4.5  Remaining relaxed

An essential component of attentiveness is being relaxed while adopting an appropriate posture. If one is not comfortable with the posture adopted then it is not possible to concentrate fully on what is being said. Therefore, it is important to take up an attentive posture in which one feels relaxed, even if this doesn't exactly follow the guidelines discussed above. Egan (1982) apparently based these guidelines on the attentive posture used by Carl Rogers in counselling sessions which were recorded on film. While this posture was comfortable for Rogers, it does not suit everyone and we should not slavishly adhere to it.

Also, there are other factors which can communicate attentiveness or the lack of it. Bolton (1979) has written about the importance of body movements, a non-distracting environment and the distance between talker and listener.

### 5.4.6  Appropriate body motion

There are two aspects of moving one's body appropriately when listening. First, it is important to avoid distracting movements such as looking at your watch, fiddling with something in your hand, fidgeting in your seat or constantly changing position. Second, it is important to move appropriately in response to the speaker, in a way mirroring the speaker's body motion. A listener who sits perfectly still, almost not blinking, can be quite unnerving and does not communicate attentiveness.

### 5.4.7 Non-distracting environment

One cannot expect to listen attentively in an environment in which there are distractions. The room used should be free from outside noise and the door should be kept closed. Telephone calls should be put on hold and if possible a 'Do not disturb' sign hung on the door. Within the room the chairs used should be comfortable and there should be no physical barrier such as a desk between speaker and listener.

### 5.4.8 Distance

The distance between speaker and listener has an impact on the level of attentiveness perceived by the speaker. If the distance is too great then it may seem that the listener does not want to get too involved in the interaction. If the distance is too small then the speaker will feel uncomfortable and this will impede the communication. Judging the optimal distance is complicated by the fact that this differs both between cultures and within each cultural group. In Western cultures a distance of about three feet is recommended but it is best to always look for signs of discomfort or anxiety in the listener and adjust the distance accordingly.

### 5.5 FIRST LEVEL LISTENING

The aim of first level listening is to help people to open up and feel comfortable about talking about their concerns, feelings and ideas. Bolton (1979) describes four skills for accomplishing this: door openers; minimal encourages; open questions; and attentive silence.

### 5.5.1 Door openers

A door opener is basically an invitation from the listener for the other person to talk about whatever is on his or her mind. People who are troubled often show signs of this, either non-verbally through their facial expressions, voice tone or body posture, or verbally through comments they make about the way they feel. The majority of people are not comfortable about getting troubled people to open up and therefore react to such signs by using the blocks to communication described earlier, such as diverting or denial of feelings.

In contrast, an effective listener uses an appropriate door opener. Door openers typically have four components:

*First*, the listener feeds back the person's body language or comment. For example, 'You look hassled' or 'You're feeling down today'.
*Second*, the listener provides an invitation to talk. For example, 'Would you like to talk about it?'
*Third*, the listener stays silent to give the other person time to open up and begin to talk.
*Fourth*, the listener uses attentiveness skills to demonstrate that he or she is paying complete attention.

It is not necessary to use all four components every time. In many situations the first step can be omitted and the process begun with an invitation to talk. Finding the right words for this invitation depends on who the talker and listener are and how well they know one another. I often use the invitation, 'How are things with you?' because it leaves the choice of whether or not to open up, and determination of the agenda, completely to the other person. Then, if people do not want to talk about their concerns at that time they can easily turn down the invitation by replying something like, 'Fine' or 'OK'. This is important since people will not always be ready to talk about their concerns. All the listener can do is provide an appropriate door opener and then leave it up to the other person. No-one likes to be coerced into talking about their concerns but if they know there is someone prepared to listen they can always take up the opportunity at a later time.

### 5.5.2 Minimal encourages

Once a person has begun to talk it is important to let them know that you are with them, in a way that does not interfere with the flow. Listeners may smile or nod their heads or use what are referred to as 'non-verbal grunts', such as 'Mm-mm', 'Yes', 'Right', and 'Go on', to encourage the speaker to continue. Other minimal encourages are slightly more intrusive but still basically supportive, for example, 'Tell me more about ...', 'And?', 'So?', 'For instance?'. A further way of encouraging the speaker to continue is when the listener repeats the last word or a key word in the speaker's statement.

### 5.5.3 Open questions

Open questions are designed to help people clarify their own concerns rather than provide information for the listener. In contrast to closed questions which typically require a one word answer such as yes or no, open questions usually start with the words, 'How?' or 'What?' and encourage a longer response. In most instances, when one is using listening skills, it will be necessary to ask some open questions. For example, when the listener is confused about what the person is saying, or what he or she really means, it is important to use open questions to provide some clarification. However, as discussed earlier in this chapter, asking too many questions, particularly closed questions, acts as a block to effective communication. In my experience, avoiding doing this is the biggest hurdle most people face when attempting to improve their listening skills. Our education system trains us in a question and answer mode of interacting with each other, and this often proves very difficult for us to get out of. Practice of the active listening skills discussed later in this chapter usually helps in this regard.

### 5.5.4 Attentive silence

Using silence appropriately is a very effective way of encouraging people to open up and continue exploring their thoughts and feelings. Research has shown that, during silences, speakers are typically clarifying their thoughts and going deeper into their feelings. Therefore, good listeners tend to pause after each thing they say to give the speaker the opportunity to carry on talking or to remain silent. However, many people in Western society are unable to leave silences, either in conversations between two people or when they are in a group. Such people feel uncomfortable with silences and will jump in to fill them, often by asking questions. In order to help people to be able to use attentive silence and thereby become better listeners Bolton (1979) suggests three things to do during a silence. First, one should continue to demonstrate attentiveness, as discussed earlier. Second, one should observe the speaker's body language very carefully. Third, one should focus on the key message which the speaker is communicating.

However, silence can be taken too far. I have seen some trainees in interpersonal skills be so unsure about what to say that they have left far too many silences. If, during a silence, the other person appears to be uncomfortable and looks at the listener for a comment, the silence should be ended, typically by using paraphrasing, which is discussed next.

## 5.6 PARAPHRASING

If paraphrasing is used along with passive listening and first level listening skills, the quality of listening overall will be improved. Paraphrasing is a skill which most people already use to some extent. When someone has told us something important and we want to be sure that we have understood correctly, we feed back the main points of the message to the person for his or her confirmation. This is a crude form of paraphrasing which is similar to that used by competent listeners. Bolton (1979) states that an effective paraphrase has four components:

> *First*, the paraphrase feeds back only the key points of the speaker's message. Less important parts of what the speaker has said are omitted, and no new ideas are added by the listener.
> *Second*, the paraphrase focuses on the speaker's thoughts rather than his or her feelings. That is, paraphrasing is concerned with the factual content of the speaker's message.
> *Third*, an effective paraphrase is short and to the point. It

is a summary of the speaker's key message, not a summary of everything said.

*Fourth*, a paraphrase is made up of the listener's own words, not a repetition of the words the speaker has used. Also, effective paraphrases are stated in language which is familiar to the speaker. For example, colloquial expressions such as, 'fed up' or 'chuffed' are particularly effective if these are commonly used by the speaker.

Paraphrases are used when there are natural breaks in the interaction, such as when the speaker pauses and looks at the listener or when the speaker inflects his or her voice at the end of a sentence, clearly wanting some response from the listener. At this point the listener feeds back the essence of the speaker's message and then waits for a response. When the paraphrase hits the mark the speaker typically indicates that this is the case by saying, 'That's it' or 'Right' or 'Yes' or by some non-verbal means such as nodding his or her head. If the paraphrase is not accurate or only partly accurate then the response will not be so positive and in most cases the speaker will correct the listener. In so doing the speaker will also be clarifying for himself or herself exactly what is meant, so the paraphrase will still have been of value.

Sometimes the listener is not sure what the speaker's key message is so does not know what to paraphrase. A suggestion in this situation is to paraphrase the last issue which the speaker has raised on the basis that people often finish with the issue that is of most importance to them.

There are five main reasons for using paraphrasing:

*First*, it shows you are really listening, because it is not possible to accurately paraphrase someone when you are not listening well;

*Second*, it is the best way of making sure you have understood correctly, and of letting the speaker know you have understood him or her;

*Third*, the act of attempting to paraphrase actually helps to stop self-listening and to reduce the risk of a communication block being used;

*Fourth*, it helps the speaker to clarify his or her thoughts;

*Fifth*, it encourages the speaker to go on exploring his or her concerns or ideas.

Many people are very unsure about using paraphrasing in this way when they first hear about it. Some consider it is artificial and feel awkward using it. Others are sceptical about whether it will work. My response is to suggest that all new skills feel awkward at first and that practice will make it become more natural and eventually automatic. I usually draw an analogy with learning to drive a car. At first it seems very awkward and concentrating on all the things you have to do tends to distract you from watching the road ahead. Whereas, with experience you can drive along without even thinking about what you are doing. I also suggest that if people are not prepared to give paraphrasing a thorough trial themselves, they will never realize its value and they will miss out on learning a skill that could significantly improve the quality of their personal and professional lives.

I have seen lots of people learn to paraphrase well within a few hours of practice, including those who were initially sceptical. It does not demand great intellectual ability, in fact I have observed that the time taken to learn paraphrasing is typically inversely related to professional status, the less highly qualified the person is the quicker he or she learns!

Paraphrasing is a skill which appears very simple and easy to use but in fact is very difficult to do well. I have found it invaluable in both my work and personal life but still feel the need to improve my skills after over 20 years of practice. Fortunately, one does not have to be an expert to put it to good use. As long as people attempt to paraphrase, rather than use the usual blocks to communication they will see positive results. This is because, unless practically every paraphrase is off the mark, speakers will use the listeners' imperfect attempts at paraphrasing to clarify their thoughts and continue to explore their concerns.

## 5.7 REFLECTING FEELINGS

Since most people who seek help to discuss concerns have strong emotions associated with those concerns it is important to be able to listen to and reflect back their feelings. Reflecting feelings is less likely to be familiar to people than the reflection of thoughts (paraphrasing) discussed above. In fact, listeners generally tend to focus on facts rather than feelings.

This is because most societies constrain people to hide their emotions, which in turn makes it more difficult for others to tune into them. However, reflecting feelings tends to help people understand their reactions to the situations with which they are faced and therefore move closer toward finding solutions to their concerns. So it is an essential component of the listening process (Bolton, 1979).

Reflecting feelings involves listeners feeding back, as concisely as possible, the feelings communicated, either verbally or non-verbally, by speakers. The format, 'You feel . . .' is usually used, for example, 'You feel angry' or 'You are annoyed' or 'You're furious'. In order to do this listeners must be able to identify feeling clues from what speakers say and from their body language. Since much of the emotional content of people's messages is communicated by their body language, it is perhaps more important to listen to what is not said than to what is said. This is why Gargiulo (1985) has suggested that reflecting feelings involves listening with a 'third ear'.

Brammer (1988) states that reflection of feelings typically has four elements:

> *First*, the feeling which the speaker is communicating is identified;
> *Second*, this feeling is reflected back to the speaker;
> *Third*, the listener carefully observes the speaker's reaction;
> *Fourth*, the listener judges the accuracy of the reflection from the reaction which he or she has observed.

As with paraphrasing, inaccurate reflection of feelings can have a facilitative effect, because the speaker corrects the listener and in so doing clarifies the emotions he or she is experiencing.

Probably the most difficult aspect of reflecting feelings is identifying the correct feeling. Bolton (1979) has suggested four things one can do to help with this:

> *First*, pick up on any words which are used to describe feelings. If these are congruent with the person's body language then they can be reflected directly. If they are not congruent then this contradiction can be fed back to the speaker. For example, 'You say you are pleased about what has happened but you actually look sad'.

*Second*, the overall content of the message may be of help in identifying the likely feelings experienced. For example, if the person is speaking about a close friend who has just died then it is likely that feelings of sadness and loss will be to the fore.

*Third*, the speaker's body language will probably provide strong clues regarding the feelings experienced. The listener should pay close attention to facial expressions, changes of body posture, tone of voice, breathing or speech, plus other aspects of body language.

*Fourth*, listeners should ask themselves, 'What would I be feeling if I were in this situation? Although different people react very differently to the same situation, the listeners' reactions may provide a useful estimate of the speaker's feelings, which can be compared with the clues gathered from the other three sources (discussed above) before feeding them back.

| FEELING | MILD | MODERATE | STRONG |
|---|---|---|---|
| Anger _____ | e.g. annoyed __ | e.g. angry _____ | e.g. furious __ |
| Happiness _____ | | | |
| Guilt _____ | | | |
| Insecurity _____ | | | |
| Embarrassment _____ | | | |
| Helplessness _____ | | | |
| Sadness _____ | | | |
| Depression _____ | | | |
| Fear _____ | | | |
| Worry _____ | | | |
| Upset _____ | | | |
| Pleasure _____ | | | |
| Frustration_____ | | | |
| Elation _____ | | | |
| Confusion _____ | | | |
| Anxiety _____ | | | |
| Love _____ | | | |
| Hate _____ | | | |
| Jealousy _____ | | | |

**Figure 5.1** Vocabulary for levels of intensity of feeling.

Finding just the right words to reflect the speaker's feelings is also very difficult. It is important to feed back the correct level of emotion as well as the type. For example, for a person expressing anger the emotional level can range from being 'slightly annoyed' to absolutely furious'. To improve one's ability to find the most appropriate vocabulary for reflecting feelings it is useful to attempt to identify words which express a range of levels of intensity for the major emotions which people experience. One way of doing this is to brainstorm words to fit the mild, moderate and strong levels of intensity of feelings, such as those listed in Fig. 5.1.

### 5.8 REFLECTING MEANINGS

The most facilitative form of reflection is the reflection of meanings. This involves reflecting both thoughts and feelings to the speaker. The speaker's key feeling is fed back along with the apparent reason for the feeling. Typically, the formula, 'You feel ... because ...' is used.

For example:

'You *feel* frustrated *because* you haven't finished the job',
'You *feel* delighted *because* she has done so well'.

When someone has learnt to paraphrase (reflect thoughts) and to reflect feelings then it does not usually take too long for them to learn to reflect meanings using the, 'You feel ... because ...' formula. Although it is common to experience the artificiality of this formula, it is useful, in the early stages of practising the skill, as an aid to producing a concise response which includes both a feeling and the reason for the feeling. Once the skill has been mastered then other words can be used instead of 'feel' and 'because' so that it becomes more natural. Examples are:

'You *are* angry *about* the way you were treated.'
You're sad *that* it has come to an end.'
'You *were* pleased *with* the result.'
'You *were* annoyed *by* her manner.'

### 5.9 ACTIVE LISTENING

Active listening is generally understood to be, 'Trying to understand what the person is feeling and what the key message is in what they are saying. Then putting this understanding into your own words and feeding it back to the person' (Gordon, 1970). Thus, active listening is taken to include all aspects of passive listening and first level listening, plus paraphrasing, reflection of feelings and reflection of meanings. That is, active listening involves the use of everything that has been discussed in this chapter. It is the most advanced and facilitative form of listening and is useful in a wide variety of situations including counselling, interviews and times when one has to be assertive. It is a skill well worth practising because the potential benefits for improving interpersonal communication and the quality of life are substantial. It is a skill that I have found invaluable in both my professional and personal life. However, until one has experienced the benefits of active listening, both as a listener and as the person being listened to it is difficult to fully appreciate its value.

A young woman on a course I once led was so uncertain about active listening that she even refused to practise it in the training group. The following week she asked if she could say something to the group. During the week a close friend had telephoned her to say that her husband was terminally ill with cancer. She said that to her surprise she found herself using active listening. The various blocks to communication we had discussed seemed totally inappropriate and all that felt comfortable was reflecting her friend's thoughts and feelings. This real life experience had convinced her of the value of active listening.

However, learning to use active listening is not without its pitfalls. There are several typical errors which people make in the early stages of learning the skill (Brammer, 1988):

*First*, there is a tendency to stereotype responses by beginning all responses with the same words, such as 'You feel ...', or 'I hear you saying ...', or 'I gather that ...' It's best to vary these and make your responses as natural as possible.

*Second*, beginners often try to get in with a listening response after each thing which the speaker has said. This is unnecessary and breaks up the speaker's flow. It is best to wait until the speaker pauses and indicates to the listener that a response is wanted. However, some people will go on and on unless you stop them, so it is important to interrupt such people so that active listening can be used to facilitate more meaningful exploration of their concerns and feelings.

*Third,* beginners often find it difficult to gauge the correct depth of concern and intensity of feeling to feed back. It is usually better to err on the side of less drastic levels of concern and less intense feelings initially. The speaker will correct this if necessary.

*Fourth,* a frequent mistake for beginners is to use language that is not commonly used by the speaker. The more listeners use the vocabulary typically used by the person they are listening to the more effective their responses will be.

### 5.10 SUMMARY

The use of empathic listening skills is regarded as essential when working with parents of children with disabilities and other members of their families. Many professionals would benefit from improving their listening skills. In this chapter the distinction between hearing and listening is clarified and the attitudes required for effective listening are described. Typical blocks to communication such as reassurance and inappropriate questioning are discussed. The components of attentiveness and first level listening, which are used in order to help people open up, are explained. The skills of para-phrasing and reflecting feelings and meanings are described in order to clarify what is involved in active listening.

In the next chapter the use of listening skills is taken a step further with a focus on the counselling skills needed to work with parents.

# 6

# Counselling skills

## 6.1 KNOWLEDGE, ATTITUDES AND SKILLS REQUIRED FOR COUNSELLING

The goals of counselling for parents of children with disabilities are somewhat different from those generally associated with psychotherapy or more in-depth counselling. Counselling for parents and other family members is not intended to bring about personality change but to help normally functioning people cope better with the additional demands of living with a child with a disability (Telford and Sawrey, 1981). Counselling is needed in order to help parents come to terms with the disability and to help them find solutions to the day to day problems presented by such children. In order to provide effective counselling and support to these parents professionals need to have certain knowledge, attitudes and skills. These are outlined below.

### 6.1.1 Knowledge

Professionals must be knowledgeable in a number of areas. First of all they should have a good understanding of human development and behaviour so that they can recognize what is within the bounds of normal behaviour and what is considered abnormal behaviour in parents and other family members (Stewart, 1986). They should be aware of how parents, siblings and members of extended families are likely to react to disabilities and how this typically affects family dynamics (Chapter 2). They should also be aware of the wide range of feelings which parents are likely to experience. Of course, professionals cannot possibly 'know how parents feel' but having had to deal with a traumatic incident in their own lives they would perhaps have experienced some of these feelings and therefore would have a better understanding of what parents are going through.

Professionals should have a good knowledge of themselves including their strengths and weaknesses related to counselling. They need to be aware of their values and in particular any prejudices they may have. They also need a good knowledge of the values, beliefs and typical behavioural patterns of members of the various cultural groups which the families they work with come from, while acknowledging the uniqueness of each family (Sue, Arredondo and McDavis, 1992). They need to know about the wide range of services for people with disabilities which are available to parents. In particular they need to know where they can refer parents when they need help which is beyond their area of expertise. Finally, they need to have a good knowledge of the counselling process and how it is likely to affect parents.

### 6.1.2 Attitudes

The most important attitudes which professionals need to have in order to effectively counsel parents are those of genuineness, respect and empathy (Rogers, 1980) which were discussed in the previous chapter. In addition, they need to be interested in other people and to get satisfaction from helping them (Stewart, 1986). They must believe that parents have the resources within them to understand their problems and adapt their behaviour in order to achieve their goals (Rogers, 1980). They need to view people as being basically friendly, dependable, self-motivated and worthy of help (Gargiulo, 1985). They should have a constructive, problem-solving approach to working with people and a belief that no problem is too big or small to warrant their attention.

### 6.1.3 Skills

It is proposed that the counselling skills needed by professionals are those involved in a problem-solving, developmental approach counselling. One in which, as Egan (1984, p. 139) suggests,

> Helpers listen to the problem situations of their clients in terms of developmental stages, tasks and crises, in terms of interactions with the social settings of life, and in terms of the strengths, deficits and unused potential in the area of life skills.

These skills are included in the counselling model which is described next.

### 6.2 THREE-STAGE COUNSELLING MODEL

The counselling model presented in this chapter is based on a general approach to counselling which can be used with children and adults in a wide variety of situations. The model involves a three-stage approach to counselling with stages of listening; understanding; and, action planning. It is a problem-solving approach to counselling which draws on previous models by Egan (1982) and Allan and Nairne (1984). In addition to using the model for general counselling, and in my work with parents of children with disabilities, I have also taught it to various groups of professionals who work with such parents in England, New Zealand, Canada and India (see Hornby, 1990; Hornby and Peshawaria, 1991). Feedback from the professionals who have used the model in their work with this group of parents suggests that it is a useful framework for providing supportive counselling.

As was suggested in Chapter 4, some parents of children with disabilities will be in need of counselling. However, the majority of these parents will not ask for counselling directly, but will typically go to a professional with a concern about the child. If the professional uses listening skills in order to help parents explore their concerns, as suggested in the previous chapter, then the parents' need for help will emerge. This is when professionals should be able to help parents by providing the counselling that they need. Parents of children with disabilities are much more likely to be willing to talk about their concerns with someone who is working directly with their child, such as a physiotherapist, nurse, psychologist or teacher than with a professional counsellor who they do not know. In my experience, most counselling of parents is carried out by professionals during intervention sessions supposedly focused on the child. The professionals involved work on the rationale that they are helping the children through their parents, which indeed they are. The fact that a wide range of professionals, including doctors, social workers and speech therapists are approached in this way is the reason I believe that all professionals who work with children with disabilities and their parents should be able to act in a counselling capacity alongside their main professional role.

What professionals who work with these parents need therefore are counselling skills embedded in a model which can be used alongside the professionals' main areas of expertise. It is considered that the model presented in this chapter is a most useful one for such professionals since it is one which can be brought into play quickly so that a counselling session can occur naurally as part of the intervention session aimed primarily at the child. This makes it more acceptable to parents and to professionals. A summary of the counselling model is presented in Fig. 6.1.

The rationale for using such a model is based on the idea that any problem or concern which parents bring to counselling can be dealt with by taking them through the three stages of the model in order to help them find the solution that best suits their family. First of all, the counsellor uses the skills of the listening stage to establish a working relationship with parents, to help them open up and to explore any concerns they have. Then the counsellor moves on to the second stage, using the skills of understanding in order to help parents get a clearer picture of their concerns, develop new perspectives on their situation, and suggest possible goals for change. Finally, the counsellor moves on to the third stage, of action planning, in which possible options for solving parents' problems are examined and plans for action are developed.

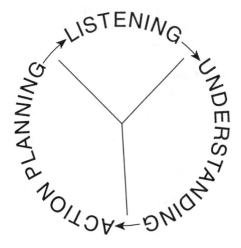

**Figure 6.1** Summary of counselling model.

The model has the flexibility to cope with a wide variety of parents' concerns and problems. For example, if the problem presented is mainly a practical one, such as dealing with the child's bed-wetting, then the counsellor could move quickly through the listening and understanding stage of the model and the majority of time could be spent on stage three, action planning. Alternatively, if the concern is mainly one which involves parents' feelings, such as their reactions to the way they were told about the disability, then the majority of time would be spent at stage one using listening skills, and the counsellor would only go on to stages two and three if this was necessary.

The circular nature of the model, as illustrated in Fig. 6.1, is important in that it emphasizes that it isn't always necessary to start at action planning and cycle back to listening. For example, if a parent is upset and is demanding immediate advice on a practical problem which has him or her highly stressed, then it is best to address this first and, when the parent has calmed down, move on to the listening stage in order to explore any concerns the parent may have. Another feature of the circular nature of the model is that it emphasizes the possibility of recyling the process, that is going back to the listening stage and working through the model again, if the action plan has not solved the parent's problems.

Over many years I have found it extremely useful to have this three-stage model in my head when working with parents of children with disabilities. The model's stages of listening, understanding and action planning provide a framework for working with such parents which is simple enough to remember under pressure yet flexible enough to deal with any problem or concern with which I have been presented. It is also a model which has proved easy to teach and quick for fellow professionals to learn. I am hopeful that, after reading this book, you too will find the model valuable in your work with parents. In order to be able to use the model you will need to be familiar with the skills involved at each stage of the three stages. A summary of the skills involved in each of the three stages of the counselling model is presented in Fig. 6.2.

## 6.3 STAGE ONE: LISTENING SKILLS

The first stage of the model involves the use of listening skills in order to help parents explore their concerns and ideas. The listening skills involved are the ones described in Chapter 5. Passive listening and first level listening are used to establish a working relationship and to help parents open up. Paraphrasing and active listening are used to help parents explore their thoughts and feelings.

Often just using active listening with people helps them express feelings and examine various thoughts, which leads to them understanding their situation better and to finding solutions to their difficulties. This has certainly been the case for me on some of the occasions when I have sought counselling from friends or professional colleagues. Active listening has been sufficient in itself to deal with my concerns and help me decide what action to take. However, on other occasions I have needed to go further than active listening alone could take me.

| Stage | 1 | 2 | 3 |
|---|---|---|---|
| SKILLS | LISTENING | UNDERSTANDING | ACTION PLANNING |
| T | *Passive Listening* | structuring | brainstorming options |
| E | complete attention | summarising | evaluating options |
| C | attentiveness skills | informing | developing plans for action |
| H | no communication blocks | self-disclosure | facilitating assertion |
| | no self-listening | you-me talk | evaluating progress |
| N | *First Level Listening* | identifying themes | re-cycling the process |
| I | door openers | expressing implications | arranging for further contact |
| Q | minimal encourages | making connections | referring on |
| U | open questions | noting contradictions | terminating contact |
| | attentive silence | suggesting alternative interpretations | |
| E | *Paraphrasing* | suggesting new perspectives | |
| S | reflecting thoughts | suggesting tentative conclusions | |
| | *Active Listening* | developing goals | |
| | reflective feelings, thoughts and meanings | | |

Direction of movement during the counselling process

**Figure 6.2** Overview of counselling model and skills.

My experience with parents of children with disabilities has been similar to my own. In many situations active listening has been both necessary and sufficient to deal with the concerns which parents have expressed. In other situations it has been necessary to go further, on to the understanding and action planning stages of the model, in order to find solutions to parents' difficulties.

Despite active listening not always being sufficient to meet parents' needs I strongly believe that it is always a necessary part of the helping process. Professionals often want to skip the listening stage and move straight on to finding solutions for parents' concerns. This is particularly true when the initial concern expressed by parents is a practical one which does not appear to involve parental feelings to any extent. However, as noted in the previous chapter, when seeking help there is a general tendency to present a minor problem first to check whether the helper can be trusted with more serious concerns. When professionals skip the listening stage their attempts at helping parents solve the problems initially presented act as a block to the exploration and communication of any more serious concerns parents may have. Therefore, I maintain that it is best to spend time taking parents through the listening stage in order to ensure that the difficulties being addressed are the ones of greatest concern to the parents. If the parent's highest priority is indeed a practical problem then it will only be necessary to spend a short time on listening before moving on. However, having used listening skills to establish a working relationship and help parents open up, professionals will not only be more confident that they are working on the parent's major concern but also will have established the rapport needed for helping parents solve their problems using the action planning stage of the model.

Another reason why listening is regarded to be of such importance that a whole chapter is devoted to it, is that some recent research suggests that professionals who have had a limited amount of training in counselling are generally more competent at the skills involved in stages two and three of the model, than they are at the skills involved in stage one, which involves listening (Hornby and Peshawaria, 1991). However, the same research showed that these professionals were able to significantly improve their listening skills in a 30-hour course. So although listening only makes up the first stage of the three-stage counselling model, it is an essential component of the helping process which must not be overlooked.

## 6.4 STAGE TWO: UNDERSTANDING SKILLS

The second stage of the model involves the use of understanding skills in order to help parents get a clearer picture of their concerns, develop new perspectives on their situation, and suggest possible goals for change. The understanding skills are described below.

### 6.4.1 Structuring

Often when parents are exploring concerns some structuring of the direction of the exploration by the counsellor is necessary. There are four main situations when this is called for. First, when what parents are saying is unclear or confusing the counsellor needs to seek clarification, perhaps by asking, 'How do you mean?' or saying, 'I'm not sure what you mean by . . .' or by asking for an example of what the parent is saying. Second, when parents bring up several problems at the same time they need to be asked to focus on the one which concerns them the most. For example, 'You have mentioned several difficulties. Could you say more about the one that concerns you most?' Third, when parents are discussing concerns in an intellectual manner and appear to be ignoring their emotional reactions they need to be asked to focus on the feelings associated with these concerns. Questions such as, 'And how does that make you feel?', or 'How do you feel about that?' can be useful. Fourth, when parents are going on and on about something and it appears to be leading nowhere, they need to be stopped and re-focused on their major concern. Probably the best way of doing this is by using summarizing, which is discussed next.

### 6.4.2 Summarizing

The skill of summarizing involves feeding back to parents a concise re-statement of the key concerns, feelings and themes they have expressed so far. It is a wide ranging form of active listening which has the effect of giving a sense of direction and achievement to the counselling process and also reassures parents that they are being listened to intently (Brammer, 1988). There are a number of times when summarizing can be useful. First, as mentioned above, when parents are talking but it appears to be leading nowhere then summarizing can provide a sense of direction and refocus them. Second, summarizing can help to provide a sense of closure to a counselling session by highlighting what has been covered and what has been learned in the session. Third, summarizing what has occurred in previous meetings can be a helpful way to begin a new counselling session with parents.

The fourth, and in actual fact, the major use of summarizing is to provide a bridge between the first and last stages of the counselling model. The summary is used to check whether parents have thoroughly explored their concerns and feelings and whether the counsellor has adequately understood these. If this is the case then the parents are likely to be gaining a better understanding of their situation and thereby moving towards considering what their options for action are. Thus, summarizing is used to move out of stage 1 (listening), into stage 2 (understanding) and prepare for movement to stage 3 (action planning).

Actually, summarizing is such a useful strategy that it can and should be used throughout the counselling process. It is almost impossible for it to be harmful whereas it is virtually universally helpful. It is my standby; if ever I'm not sure what to do or where to go I summarize!

It is also worth mentioning that it can be helpful in some situations to get parents themselves to summarize, particularly in stage 3 when plans of action are being developed.

### 6.4.3 Informing

There are many occasions when professionals can beneficially pass on information to parents. Most often this is related to their own area of expertise, for example speech therapists may give parents information about language development, social workers may inform parents about services available. On other occasions the information required may not be in the professional's area and there may be a need to discuss how it can be obtained. A third type of information which is often of interest to parents is related to the normality or otherwise of their reactions. For example, as noted in Chapter 2, parents find it valuable to know about the typical effects of the grieving process on themselves and other members of their families. To be told by a professional that it is quite normal to experience intense feelings of anger and sadness is a great relief to many parents. The skill of informing comes at stage 2 of the model because if such information were provided to parents before they had undergone the listening undertaken in stage 1 it could act as a communication block. In contrast, it is often helpful for various types of information to be provided at stage 3.

### 6.4.4 Self-disclosure

Many professionals have been taught during their training that they must not tell parents anything about themselves or ever show their feelings. The rationale for this is to keep professionals at a distance from parents and thereby maintain their status. However, this approach is not acceptable when one is attempting to establish working relationships based on genuineness and trust, which is necessarily the case in counselling. I have certainly found that it helps to share something of myself with parents. This is my general policy in counselling since I agree with Rogers (1980) that genuineness is a key factor in establishing effective counselling relationships. Thus, briefly disclosing something about oneself is a good way to foster this. Therefore, where it is clearly relevant to what is being discussed and I consider that it will be helpful, I briefly disclose to parents such things as the fact that I had a stammer as a child and have been divorced twice. Not things which I'm particularly proud of, but ones which make it clear that I am human too.

### 6.4.5 You–me talk

Another skill which requires a certain amount of courage from professionals is one which Egan (1982) has called 'You–me talk'. This involves checking with the parent about what is happening in the counselling relationship itself. It may be that the counsellor has detected some irritation on the part of the parent that he or she considers may be holding back progress. If this is the case then the counsellor would say something like, 'You seem to be a little irritated. Is it about something which I've said or done?' This typically leads to the parent opening up about what is bothering him or her which then frees up the counselling relationship for further progress.

Checking out what is going on in the parent–professional relationship in this way is always a useful thing to do if the professional detects tension in the relationship. In many instances parents' feelings will be found not to be related to anything the professional has said but to other issues which are bothering parents, which can then be fruitfully explored. However, on some occasions it is something which the professional has said that has upset the parent. If the professional receives this feedback then it is important that he or she does not get defensive but uses active listening skills in order to help parents express their feelings and thereby dissipate the tension.

### 6.4.6 Identifying themes

An important part of helping parents gain a better under-standing of their current situation and concerns is to point out any themes, or common threads, which appear to be running through parents' stories but which they do not seem to be aware of. For example, a theme which seems to run through many of the accounts of parents with mentally handicapped children is concern about the care of their children in the future when they become old, ill or die. If this is an issue which a parent keeps coming back to then it should be pointed out to him or her that it is apparently a major concern.

### 6.4.7 Expressing implications

This involves pointing out the implications or possible conse-quences of what the parent is saying or of a theme which has emerged. To take the example above, if it has emerged that the future care of the child is a major concern then the implication which needs to be communicated to the parent is that this concern needs to be addressed. The various options can then be examined in stage 3 of the model. One way of stating this might be, 'It seems that your major worry is about who will look after her when you're no longer able to .... Shall we talk about some of the options?'

Another example is when parents express great concern about the marital difficulties caused by their child with a disability. The implications of this are that, if it is allowed to continue, it could split up the marriage. This needs to be sensitively communicated to the parents in a way which moves them on to considering their various options in stage 3 of the model. For example, 'You seem to be concerned that if these problems are allowed to continue they could pose a threat to your marriage ... Would you like to talk about what can be done about it?'

### 6.4.8 Making connections

Parents will often express thoughts or feelings at different times during a counselling session which appear to be linked. However, they may not have realized the connection, so it is the professional's job to point this out. For example, some parents will be experiencing the symptoms of stress which from what they say is fairly clearly due to the extra demands of caring for their disabled children. It would be valuable for professionals who note this link to help parents to make this connection. They could say something like, 'Have you thought about the possibility that these symptoms you are having could be your body's reactions to the heavy demands of caring for your child'. This could then lead on to considering the various options available in stage 3 of the model.

### 6.4.9 Noting contradictions

There will sometimes be discrepancies between thoughts and feelings expressed by parents at different times during the session. Sometimes parents will appear to contradict what they have said earlier in the session. On other occasions what parents say appears to contradict the feelings they are expressing. In both these cases these discrepancies should be pointed out to parents to enable them to achieve a better understanding of their ideas and feelings. For example, 'You have said that you are pleased with the assessment results but you look disappointed'.

### 6.4.10 Suggesting alternative interpretations

This skill is one that is used a lot in everyday life and is therefore a skill at which most people are fairly good. It involves suggesting different possible explanations for what has already happened, that is, it focuses on the past. For example, parents often wonder if they are responsible for causing their child's disability. In some societies there are unhelpful myths about the aetiology of disability, such as in traditional Samoan culture it is believed that children born with disabilities are the result of the father having had an extramarital affair. When a Samoan family turned up in New Zealand with three blind children the professionals who worked with them were able to give the parents an alternative explanation of the aetiology based on genetics.

### 6.4.11 Suggesting new perspectives

This skill is also widely used in everyday lfe. It involves helping people to consider new ways of looking at the problem situation they are concerned about. That is, to think of more constructive ways of viewing things. Egan (1990) has referred to this skill as 'creating new scenarios'. He suggests that clients be involved in this process by asking questions like, 'How would things look if they were to seem better?'

Attempting to help clients take a more positive and constructive perspective of their situation has a long history in counselling and is the basis of the approaches of several well known theorists (e.g. Beck, 1976; Ellis, 1974). When it works it can be extremely helpful, but it is also a high-risk strategy, as the professional, mentioned in the previous chapter, who suggested that parenting a child with a disability can be character building, found out. If used too early in the counselling process, before considerable use has been made of listening and understanding skills, then it can act as a block to communication.

### 6.4.12 Suggesting tentative conclusions

To round off stage 2 and prepare for moving into stage 3 of the model it is helpful for professionals to check that the discussion is focusing on the parents' major concern. In order to do this the professional could say, for example, 'Am I right in thinking that your biggest worry at present is his behaviour at home?' If this is not correct then the professional will need to continue to work with stage 2 skills and perhaps even go back to stage 1 skills to clarify the parents' views. If the parents reply in the affirmative then it suggests that they are almost ready to move on to stage 3 of the model.

### 6.4.13 Developing goals

This skill is usually used when the parent is almost ready to move on to stage 3 of the model. Once the parent's major concerns have been identified and some views obtained of how things might be different then the counsellor can help parents decide what they want to change. That is, parents can develop their goals.

### 6.5 STAGE THREE: ACTION PLANNING SKILLS

The third stage of the model involves the use of action planning skills in order to help parents consider possible options for solving their problems and to develop plans for action. The action planning skills are described below.

### 6.5.1 Brainstorming options

Usually when people have a concern which has bothered them sufficiently to seek help, they have thought of what they would like to do about it, but are often reluctant to mention this for fear of a negative reaction from the helper. So when I am counselling parents and have worked through stages 1 and 2 of the model, I will often move into stage 3 by saying, 'Have you thought of what you might do about it?' Alternatively,

I sometimes ask, 'What options have you got?' These open questions are aimed at getting parents thinking about the possible options available to them.

Even if the options which parents bring up seem that they would provide adequate solutions to their problems it is most often a good idea to encourage parents to come up with other potential solutions. It may well be that a more satisfactory solution can be found from this wider range of options. Brainstorming is a technique which can be used to generate more options. The idea is to get parents to think of as many ways as possible of solving their problems. No evaluation of the options is allowed at first; all suggestions are accepted. When parents start to dry up they are then asked to think of some 'crazy' solutions in order to facilitate more creative problem-solving. This usually leads to some humorous solutions being suggested and occasionally thoughts are triggered which lead to an excellent practicable potential solution to the problem.

Finally, if I am not happy with the options generated by the parents or I consider there are others which may well be better than those suggested by the parents, I will suggest some potential solutions myself. Clearly, it is better if parents can complete the problem-solving process by themselves since they are likely to be more committed to an action plan based on their own ideas and there is less risk of encouraging dependency on the helper. However, I do not believe it is sensible to let parents continue through stage 3 with a less than adequate range of options to consider. We would not allow parents to implement a solution that could endanger their children or themselvs so why should we allow them to go forward with solutions unlikely to be successful. Parents raising children with disabilities have too much on their plates to be forced to learn by their mistakes when professionals could help out with a few suggestions.

### 6.5.2 Evaluating options

Once parents have produced a number of potential solutions to their problems the next task is to help them to select the most appropriate solution by evaluating each of the options in turn. Parents are asked to think of the likely consequences of implementing each of the potential solutions by asking such questions as, 'What is likely to happen if you do that?', 'What could go wrong and how could you handle it?' Parents are then helped to weigh up the pros and cons of each of the options and by this means to select the solution which is most likely to fulfil their goal.

Of course, it may well be that the parents decide to do nothing, as none of the options offer benefits which outweigh the potential negative consequences of implementing them. Or parents may not be able to make up their minds and need to be given time to think things over. In each of these cases the professional would need to arrange to meet with the parents on another occasion to re-cycle the counselling process.

### 6.5.3 Developing plans for action

Most professionals would consider the counselling process completed when parents have decided what action to take, and it is true that some parents would need no more help. Many parents, however, need the process to be taken further. Once parents have decided on the option they want to take the professional can then help them to develop a plan to implement the solution. Professionals can help parents to work out exactly what action they are going to take, when they are going to act, with whom they are going to discuss it, how they are going to follow it up and when they are going to review its effectiveness.

### 6.5.4 Facilitating assertion

Many parents will need no further help once the action plan has been worked out. Others, however, benefit from support from professionals in actually carrying out their action plan. Parents may lack confidence in their ability to see the plan of action through to completion. Professionals therefore need to help parents develop the necessary assertive strategies. This may involve teaching parents assertion skills and possibly using role play to get parents to rehearse what they need to do to implement the action plan. Assertion skills are the subject of the following chapter.

### 6.5.5 Evaluating progress

Professionals should ensure that the details of how progress towards the parents' goals is to be evaluated is built into the action plan. Progress can then be evaluated when parents and professionals next meet and decisions made about the possibility of further action.

### 6.5.6 Re-cycling the process

If it appears that the solution is not working then the whole process should be re-cycled. That is, the professional should take parents back to stage 1 of the counselling model in order to explore their difficulties, concerns and feelings about these. The professional should then continue through stage 2 to help parents develop a new understanding of their situation. Finally, stage 3 skills should be used to help parents develop and implement a new plan of action.

### 6.5.7 Arranging for further contact

At the end of each session the professional should arrange for further contact at the most suitable interval for checking on the parent's progress towards his or her goals. When parents are experiencing great difficulties then contact should be at least weekly, but this can be lengthened when things are looking more positive. In some situations parents may prefer to contact, or be contacted by, professionals by telephone.

### 6.5.8 Referring on

There will be situations when the professional considers that the counselling which parents need is beyond their level of competence. Although it is considered that through using this three-stage model of counselling professionals should be able to deal with the majority of parents' problems there will be some situations when more specialist help is needed. It is then the professional's responsibility to help parents to find the appropriate counselling help. For example, if it turns out that parents are mainly concerned about marital problems which are not related to their children with disabilities then professionals should refer them to qualified marriage guidance counsellors.

### 6.5.9 Terminating contact

Professionals should always end a meeting or series of meetings with parents by 'leaving the door open' for further contacts. Knowing that they can contact professionals if they experience problems in the future can be a great comfort to parents even if they never need to take this up. If professionals have been counselling parents in relation with their role of providing treatment to the child, then they can make it clear that they will continue to see the child as necessary and that parents should feel able to raise their own concerns whenever they need to.

### 6.6 SUMMARY

Providing supportive counselling to parents is an important function of all professionals who work with children with disabilities and their families. The knowledge, attitudes and skills required by professionals in order to carry out such counselling are outlined in this chapter and a three-stage problem solving model of the counselling process is described. Stage 1 of the model focuses on listening skills, especially active listening, which was discussed in the previous chapter. Stage 2 involves the use of understanding skills such as summarizing and suggesting new perspectives. Stage 3 consists of action planning skills such as brainstorming options and facilitating assertion. Assertion skills are the subject of the next chapter.

# 7

---

# Assertion skills

## 7.1 NEED FOR ASSERTION SKILLS

There are three ways in which assertiveness is important for professionals working with parents of children with disabilities. First, professionals need to use assertion skills when providing guidance for parents, such as making suggestions to parents about working on intervention programmes with their children at home. Second, professionals need to be able to help parents improve their assertion skills in order to obtain the best possible services for their children. For instance, it was noted by both parents whose stories are told in Chapter 3 that they had been forced to become more assertive in order to get adequate help for their children. Third, professionals need to develop assertion skills with their colleagues in order to act as advocates for the children and parents with whom they work. There are many occasions in the disability field when there are disagreements as to the best course of action to take. Professionals should be able to assertively state their views about how children's needs can best be met.

In addition to these factors there is also the point that developing assertion skills helps people to function more effectively overall which therefore benefits all of their personal and professional relationships. It is in this wider context that I first got involved in teaching assertion skills and it is only in the last few years that I have seen their value for parents who have children with disabilities.

I got involved in teaching assertion skills in New Zealand in 1980 when I was asked to take an adult education class on the topic. I will never forget the experience. The participants were adults from very varied backgrounds. On the first of the eight evenings we met I asked everyone to come up with something specific they wanted to achieve by the time the course ended. One middle-aged woman knew immediately what her goal was. She had bought a roll of curtain material, then once she had got it home decided she no longer liked it, but now felt unable to take it back. On several occasions during the course we used this problem in order to try out different assertion techniques, role playing various ways in which it could be handled, but she was still very unsure about taking it back. Then, at the final session of the course, when participants were reporting back on their projects, she triumphantly announced that she had returned the roll of material and exchanged it for another with which she was very happy. When I asked how she had done this, she explained that she simply walked into the shop, put the material on the counter, said she wanted to exchange it, and stated firmly, 'It's no good arguing with me because I've just done a course of assertion training'!

Teaching this course convinced me of the value of assertion training. I hope reading this chapter will enable you to assert yourself more confidently and achieve some of the goals you have felt tentative about in the past. I also hope it will convince you of the value of helping parents of children with disabilities to become more assertive.

## 7.2 DEFINITION OF ASSERTIVENESS

There is no agreed definition of assertiveness in the literature on this topic but there are several common themes which run through the definitions which most writers use. These are:

- being able to stand up for one's own rights while respecting the rights of others;
- being able to communicate one's ideas, concerns and needs directly, persistently and diplomatically;
- being able to express both positive and negative feelings with openness and honesty;
- being able to choose how to react to situations from a range of options.

Assertiveness can be distinguished from three other types of reactions to situations: passive; indirect; and, aggressive. These approaches are described below.

### 7.2.1 Passive

This is a reaction in which one says and does nothing and suppresses one's feelings about whatever has happened. It is a submissive response to situations, in which people have difficulty standing up for their rights and as a consequence lack confidence in themselves.

### 7.2.2 Indirect

In this approach nothing is said directly, but negative comments are made which the person involved is meant to overhear, or facial expressions are used to convey displeasure. It is a form of indirect aggression which is intended to make the other person feel uneasy or guilty and thereby manipulate them into changing their behaviour.

### 7.2.3 Aggressive

This reaction is one in which people are only concerned with getting their own way without any consideration of the feelings or needs of others. It involves a desire to win at all costs which is what sets it apart from assertion.

### 7.2.4 Assertive

An assertive reaction is one in which people stand up for their rights and express their feelings but do these things in ways which respect the rights and feelings of others. Assertive people feel good about themselves. They see themselves as being on an equal level with others and are not afraid of conflict, criticism or confrontation. They are able to take risks and make choices based on their own needs and feelings.

### 7.2.5 Continuum of reactions

These four reactions to situations can be considered to be on a continuum from passive to aggressive with indirect and assertive in the middle. In my conceptualization of the reactions I have made the continuum into a circle to demonstrate the close link between passive and aggressive. This is illustrated in Fig. 7.1. The link is important because it reminds us that the continual use of the passive approach tends to build up

**Figure 7.1** Continuum of reactions to situations.

suppressed emotion which eventually leads to an explosion into aggressive behaviour.

The circular representation illustrates visually the fact that we have a range of options for the way we react to situations. There are pros and cons for all four reactions. However, I consider that in most situations assertive behaviour is likely to be the most effective response. But I don't deny that there are some situations in which the potential negative consequences of being assertive outweigh the potential benefits and a passive response is preferred. This is especially so when we are interacting with people who we are not going to see on a long-term basis. It is sometimes just not worth the effort of being assertive in this situation.

In other situations, in which assertion has not achieved your goals, aggressive responses are justified if the benefits will outweigh the negative consequences. New Zealanders have an expression which I like to think of when I am faced with this problem. It's called 'jumping up and down' and I like to think of it at the times when being assertive has not got the message across and an aggressive response can be justified. At these times one needs to (metaphorically) 'jump up and down' to get one's point across. It's an approach I like to have in reserve as a last resort for situations in which I consider my rights have been violated.

Ideally, we should have all four reactions within our repertoires but realize that assertive responses will be the most appropriate on most occasions. The benefits of being assertive for as much of the time as possible include the fact that one's sense of self-worth is increased. Assertive people tend to feel better about themselves than passive and aggressive individuals. Also, assertion fosters more fulfilling relationships, both with family members and with colleagues. In addition, levels of anxiety and apprehension are reduced when people become more assertive. Finally, more of a person's needs will be met by being assertive than by being passive, indirect or aggressive (Bolton, 1979).

However, there is a price to pay for being assertive. First, it takes more effort and time to be assertive than to use any of the other three responses. Second, it can be quite painful and exhausting to choose to resolve conflicts rather than walk away from them. Third, it can and does change relationships and the way you feel about them. For example, deciding to be assertive can occasionally leave people feeling dissatisfied with the quality of their marriages, which may present problems if their partners are not prepared to do anything about it. Fourth, other people may not be able to cope with you becoming more assertive. A boss may feel threatened by you being assertive and try to get rid of you. Finally, it is not easy to change the habits of a lifetime and it will take hard work on your part to become more assertive. But if you think about it, you are changing gradually all the time without realizing it. All your relationships with family members and colleagues are either improving and becoming more fulfilling or deteriorating and becoming more conflictual. So you may as well make a definite decision to change yourself positively. Then every interaction you have with another individual will be an opportunity to build a more positive relationship rather than to allow it to deteriorate.

## 7.3 ASSERTIVE RIGHTS

To be assertive one needs to have the appropriate attitudes, that is one needs to believe in certain fundamental rights of human beings. A few years ago Jakobuwski and Lange (1978) produced a list of eleven basic assertive rights which I since have found useful in teaching assertion skills. These assertive rights are described below.

### 7.3.1 The right to be treated with respect

This is a fundamental human right. No one should allow himself or herself to be the subject of abuse whether it is physical, mental or verbal. For example, we should never allow anyone to speak to us in a sarcastic or unpleasant manner or in a way which acts as a 'put down'.

### 7.3.2 The right to self-fulfilment which does not violate the rights of others

Everyone should be able to strive to become what they aspire to as long as this doesn't get in the way of other people's self-fulfilment. For example, we should not feel guilty about taking time out from our family responsibilities to work towards our own individual goals.

### 7.3.3 The right to experience and express your feelings

The delightful book, *Your Feelings are your Friends* (Knight, 1978) explains that all of our feelings are there for a purpose. For example, anger is there to give us determination to deal with difficult situations. Guilt is there to let us know when we have fallen foul of our own standards. Experiencing all your feelings and expressing them appropriately (which is discussed later in this chapter) does not violate the rights of other people.

### 7.3.4 The right to take time to think about things

Often when we are asked to do something we feel under pressure to give our answer immediately. But this is sometimes unreasonable as we may need time to think things over before we commit ourselves.

### 7.3.5 The right to change your mind

Everyone changes their mind about things from time to time but many people feel they cannot go back on what they have said they will do. This then means that they will go ahead with something they do not feel comfortable about. As my lady with the curtain material found out, other people are most often understanding about changes of mind because it happens to them too.

### 7.3.6 The right to ask for what you want

Many people feel it is selfish behaviour to ask for what you want but as long as you accept that other people have the right to turn you down it is far better to be clear about it.

### 7.3.7 The right to ask for information

Many people feel uneasy about asking for information because they think they should know the answers and will appear stupid if they ask. For example, parents are often reluctant to ask professionals for information about their children with disabilities. But this is not sensible because the vast majority of professionals are willing to give parents all the information they want and do not expect them to be knowledgeable about everything.

### 7.3.8 The right to do less than you are capable of

Perfectionism is so widespread that it is a great relief when people accept that they can choose not to go all out on something. For example, it is possible to work less than 100% on an assignment but still feel good about it when it's finished because you have other priorities.

### 7.3.9 The right to make mistakes

Everyone makes mistakes, it's just that some people feel that they are worth less because they have made an error. Our self-worth should not be threatened because we have made a mistake. We should feel pleased to be reminded that we are human. As the saying goes, 'To err is human, to forgive is divine'.

### 7.3.10 The right to say 'no' without feeling guilty

Many people find it difficult to say 'no' because they fear they may hurt the other person's feelings or let them down and this may damage their relationship with that person. But the alternative is to go ahead and feel resentful about doing something you'd rather not do. The negative feelings you have about this will probably be unconsciously communicated to the other person and do far more damage to the relationship than simply saying 'no' in the first place.

### 7.3.11 The right to feel good about yourself

People cannot give of their best if they do not feel good about themselves. Alternatively, people function far more effectively when they have a high level of self-esteem. It is therefore in everyone's interest for you to feel good about yourself. Psychologists like Ellis (1974) and Beck (1976) have emphasized the necessity of challenging negative thoughts such as, 'It's probably my fault', 'Perhaps it's not my place to say anything', and 'They'll think I'm stupid'. If one has such negative thoughts then it is impossible to be assertive. It is therefore important to replace such thoughts with statements based on the eleven assertive rights discussed above.

### 7.4 BASIC ELEMENTS OF ASSERTIVENESS

There are three aspects of assertiveness which apply in any situation. These are: physical assertiveness; vocal assertiveness; and, assertion muscle levels.

### 7.4.1 Physical assertiveness

Assertive body language is a key component of effective assertion. In many ways the components of physical assertiveness are similar to those of the attentiveness required for effective listening: an open posture, facing the other person squarely, standing or sitting erect or leaning slightly forward, good eye contact and no fidgeting or superfluous gestures. What is different is that your facial expession should match your message and your feet should be firmly planted on the floor, even if you are sitting (Bolton, 1979).

### 7.4.2 Vocal assertiveness

To optimize the effectiveness of the message your voice should be firm but calm. Speak a little more slowly than usual but at a normal volume. Make sure that you breathe deeply as this will help you stay calm as well as ensuring you have enough breath to speak firmly.

### 7.4.3 Assertion muscle levels

Whenever you are being assertive it is important to select the appropriate strength or 'muscle level' of the assertive response you use. An analogy is made with the muscle levels one uses to, say, unscrew the lid of a jar. First, one uses a low muscle level because you expect the lid to come off easily. Then, if this doesn't work, you increase the amount of muscle power and try again. Finally, if you've still had no success, you gather up your energy to give it one last burst on maximum muscle power, before passing it on to someone else for a try!

A similar approach should be used in situations which require assertion. First, you should start at the lowest muscle level or assertion strength which is likely to achieve success. For example, 'I would appreciate it if you could . . .'. If this doesn't work you should be prepared to increase the muscle levels until you get a satisfactory response. For example, from 'It is essential that you . . .' to finally, 'I demand that you . . .'.

While you are increasing muscle levels verbally, as illustrated above, you should also make your physical and vocal assertiveness gradually more intense. For example, using a more serious facial expression and a firmer tone of voice with each increase in muscle level.

### 7.5 REFUSING A REQUEST

One thing which almost everyone has difficulty with at some time or other is turning down requests made to them, in other words, saying 'no'. As a professional working with children with disabilities and their families you will sometimes receive requests from parents or other professionals which you think you shouldn't agree to but feel unable to turn down. The reasons people have difficulty saying 'no' include: thinking they must always help others; not wanting to appear selfish; feeling flattered to be asked; not wanting to hurt people's feelings; and, most importantly, fear that it will damage the relationship. So when most people turn down a request they typically offer excuses and apologies rather than give a straight 'no'. This tends to sound evasive and leaves both people feeling dissatisfied with the interaction. The alternative is to use acceptable ways of saying 'no', several of which are discussed below (Bolton, 1979).

### 7.5.1 The explained 'no'

When you have a genuine reason for the refusal you can say 'no', explain why you are turning down the request, and give a brief apology. For example, 'No, I'm sorry, I can't make it because I'm already booked for that day'.

Most people find it easier to say 'no' when they have a good reason, but much more difficult to turn down a request when they do not have a specific reason. It is best to explain this when you say 'no', that is, to say that you don't have a reason but that you really don't want to do it. For example, 'I will have to say 'no', not for any specific reason, but I just don't want to take it on'.

### 7.5.2 The postponed 'no'

In this refusal you explain that you can't comply with the request at present but may be able to in the future. For example, 'No, I'm sorry, I'm not able to take that on today, but I may be able to help you with it in the future'.

### 7.5.3 The delayed 'no'

My ability to say 'no' increased by a quantum leap when I learned how to use this technique. Often when people ask us to do things we are busy with something and are liable to agree to the request so we can get on with what we are doing. What we should do in this situation is to ask for time to think it over. For example, 'I'm busy right now and I'd like to give it some thought. Can I get back to you tomorrow?'

This then gives us the opportunity to carefully consider whether we want to comply with the request. If it is decided not to then we have time to work out exactly how we are going to say 'no'.

### 7.5.4 The listening 'no'

With this refusal active listening skills are used to let the other person know that you understand their request and any feelings they have expressed. The listening response is combined with a brief apology and a firm refusal. For example, 'Yes I understand your frustration about not being able to get the job done; I'm sorry, but I can't help you with it'.

### 7.5.5 The 'get back to me' 'no'

This is a strategy I have found to be quite useful on several occasions. It involves explaining the difficulties you have in complying with the request, suggesting that the person try elsewhere and if all else fails to come back to you and you'll see what you can do. This way you are taken to be very reasonable but overloaded and people seldom come back to you. For example, 'I'm booked up for the next two weeks so I suggest you try elsewhere; if you really get stuck I'll do my best to fit you in but I can't promise anything'.

### 7.5.6 The 'broken record' 'no'

This is a form of refusal which is particularly useful for dealing with people who won't take 'no' for an answer. It involves making a brief statement of refusal to the other person, avoiding getting into discussion with them, and simply repeating the statement as many times as necessary (like a broken record) until the message gets across. For example:

> *Refuser:* 'I'm sorry but I'm not able to help you.'
> *Requester:* 'But why not, it won't take you long?'
> *Refuser:* 'As I said, I'm not able to help you.'
> *Requester:* 'But you've done things like this for other people, why won't you do it for me?'
> *Refuser:* 'That's irrelevant. As I said, I'm not able to help you.'

Usually the message needs repeating only twice before the other person gives up, but for some people the record needs to play a little longer! In the end this strategy never fails, but it is an approach which borders on the aggressive, so it should only be used when necessary.

### 7.6 MAKING A REQUEST

Parents often need to make requests of professionals who work with their disabled children but sometimes feel diffident about doing so. Helping parents to learn how to make requests assertively is therefore a very useful function which professionals can fulfil. Also, professionals sometimes need to request various things from their colleagues and occasionally need to make requests of parents. So, being able to make requests effectively is an important issue for professionals. However, asking someone to do something for us is difficult for most people and particularly so for those who have low self-esteem and lack confidence in themselves, which may be the case for some parents. Of course, it depends on such things as how well we know the person, whether we have done something for them recently and on how much of a nuisance it is going to be to them. However, whatever the situation there are ways of increasing the chances of success, without damaging your relationship with the other person. Manthei (1981) has provided some useful guidelines for making requests and these are outlined below.

### 7.6.1 State your request directly

Use physical and vocal assertiveness to make your request firmly and clearly to the appropriate person. It is best to write out the request beforehand and rehearse it either with another person or if this is not possible in front of a mirror. Then decide on the best time and place to deliver your request. Remember that people are more likely to agree to requests at certain times such as, when they are relaxed, when they are in a good mood and after they have eaten. Therefore, try to pick the best time and place to make your request.

### 7.6.2 Say exactly what you want

Be specific and precise about your requirements. Don't underestimate or exaggerate your needs. Don't include any superfluous information. Stick to the point.

### 7.6.3 Focus on the positive

Create an expectation of compliance. Not, 'I don't suppose you could . . .' but 'Please could you . . .'. Let the person know you expect them to be able to help you and if possible, acknowledge their importance. For example, 'I've heard you're the expert on . . .' or, 'You've been very helpful to me in the past'.

### 7.6.4 Answer only questions seeking clarification

Don't allow yourself to be side-tracked into a discussion about the merits of your case. Answer clarification questions briefly and repeat the request if necessary.

### 7.6.5 Allow the person time to think about it

If the person is uncertain about complying with your request it is better to offer him or her time to think about it. For example, 'Would you like time to think it over? I could get back to you tomorrow'.

### 7.6.6 Repeat the request

Use the 'broken record' technique to restate the request using a higher 'muscle level' (see sections 7.4.3 and 7.5.6).

### 7.6.7 Be prepared to compromise

You are better off getting partial agreement than rejection. Also, once a person has agreed to part of your request they are much more likely to agree to the rest of it if you come back to them at some stage in the future.

### 7.6.8 Realize the other person has the right to refuse

Using assertion effectively does not guarantee success because you accept that the other person has rights too. However, it does allow you to feel satisfied that you have made the best possible case for your request.

## 7.7 RESPONDING TO AGGRESSION

Due to the nature of the work, which is often controversial and highly charged with emotion, professionals who work with children with disabilities and their parents will occasionally be the subject of verbal aggression. This can come from parents who feel aggrieved about some issue concerning their child or from disagreement with another professional about their assessment of or intervention with the child. It is therefore useful for professionals to have strategies for coping with this aggression. There are four strategies which are useful in dealing with verbal aggression. These are empathic assertion and fogging (Cotler and Guerra, 1976); selective ignoring and assertive withdrawal (Bolton, 1979). These are described below.

### 7.7.1 Empathic assertion

This is the best strategy for responding to someone who may be justifiably angry but is perhaps venting their aggression on the wrong person. This can sometimes happen to parents of children with disabilities. The parents may have been angered or frustrated by a professional contact in the past and feel so negatively about further professional contacts that their aggressive responses are easily triggered. As was noted in Chapters 2 and 3, many parents are angry about the way they were told about the disability, which can sour their future relationships with professionals. Also discussed in these chapters was the process of adaptation to the disability which explains that parents can react with intense feelings such as anger and frustration at various times. In addition, it is of course always possible that the professional has said or done something which has a parent justifiably angry. Given all of these factors it is clearly important that professionals who work with this group of parents can respond to anger or aggression from parents in a way which defuses the tension and yet deals with parents' concerns. I have found what I call empathic assertion the best strategy for doing this.

Empathic assertion basically involves using the active listening skills which were discussed in Chapter 6. The person who is on the receiving end of the aggression identifies the feelings and key message in what the aggressor is communicating and feeds it back to him or her. This confirms that you are not only listening but also that you understand the parent's concern and feelings. For example, 'You object to what I did and you are angry about it'. This first reflection sometimes encourages aggressors to express their feelings more strongly. When this happens a second reflection, such as, 'You're extremely angry about it', usually helps defuse the situation and makes the person more receptive to your views. Active listening should continue to be used until the aggressors are convinced they have got their point across and have calmed down. Then you can assertively express your views about the situation. If the other person starts to become aggressive again active listening can be used to restore the communication.

### 7.7.2 Selective ignoring

This is a technique mainly used for dealing with verbal abuse such as sarcasm or comments intended to put the other person down. It involves informing the other person that you object to their abusive comments and firmly requesting them to stop these immediately. If the abuse continues, you tell them that you will not participate in any communication in which he or she is abusive. If the person still continues to be abusive then you ignore them. If they ask why you're remaining silent you simply repeat your condition for talking with them. When the other person begins to speak to you without being abusive you should participate in the conversation and make a point of being particularly civil.

Selective ignoring works when used persistently because it ensures that the other person is not reinforced for behaving abusively. However, if the abuse has gone on for some time and the abuser is used to you responding passively, it will take longer to extinguish and may even increase for a short time after you begin to use selective ignoring. This initial increase in the negative response following a change in your behaviour is something which occurs fairly frequently when you are beginning to be more assertive. The other person has been used to you reacting a certain way and is 'pulling out all the stops' to get you to continue. With determination and persistence this period will soon pass as the other person 'gets the message'.

### 7.7.3 Fogging

This is a technique for 'fobbing off' aggressive or highly critical people who you don't want to spend time dealing with. It involves weakly agreeing with their comments by saying such things as 'You may be right', or 'I possibly did do that'.

A colleague of mine once nearly drove our secretary insane by using a variant of this technique. Apparently, an urgent report, which my colleague was to write, was overdue. However, every time the secretary asked her for the report the colleague would admit she hadn't done it, be very apologetic, go on about how hopeless she was and promise to have it done the next day. The following day virtually the same conversation would be repeated. Eventually, the secretary gave up asking. It's not that I'm recommending this as a way to annoy your secretary, but I do suggest that it demonstrates the power of the technique of fogging.

### 7.7.4 Assertive withdrawal

Most people know someone who is extremely aversive to deal with. Virtually every interaction with such people includes an instance of them being abusive or making a statement designed to put the other person down. One can only feel sad about the low self-esteem and inadequate personalities which lead to such behaviour. However, having to interact with these people on a regular basis is extremely stressful and we all know of cases in which people have resigned in order to avoid working with such people.

If you have to work with someone like this then the first thing to try is to use assertion skills, such as selective ignoring, to deal with their abusive behaviour. This will not be an easy assignment but, in my experience, some aversive people will respond to very high muscle level assertions and change their behaviour. Others will accept that they cannot be abusive to the asserter while continuing to behave 'as normal' with everyone else. Still others will not change their aversive manner in response to effective assertion no matter how long it is applied. It is with such people that one has to seriously consider whether the most appropriate assertion is to withdraw as much as possible from interactions with the person. This could perhaps be achieved by working out ways to avoid contact with the aversive person as much as possible. If this does not work then complete withdrawal from interaction with the person may be necessary. This may mean not doing one's job as effectively as one could or even changing jobs. You have to ask yourself whether the stress of interacting with such an aversive person on a long-term basis is really worth it.

## 7.8 RESPONDING TO CRITICISM

Everyone has experienced criticism at one time or another. Professionals who work in the disability field will occasionally get criticism from their colleagues and sometimes from parents or other family members. Criticism is a controversial topic with me because I'm uncertain about whether it is a valuable strategy or not. There have been times in my life when I have found criticism to be extremely helpful and other times when I have found it to be incredibly destructive. Two incidents from my past immediately spring to mind.

The first incident occurred when a colleague was extremely critical of a project I was working on. I thought about it over-night and decided that I had a choice, I could either reject the criticism and avoid this person in the future or I could go back to him and ask for specific suggestions of how he would change the project. I decided to do the latter, found him very helpful and the project was significantly improved by his suggestions. We became friends and he has since been a great help to me with certain aspects of my career.

The second incident occurred when I was studying in Vancouver. About half way through the academic year there was tremendous conflict within the group I was in. I decided to bring this into the open and attempt to resolve it during a seminar we all had together. In the event, most of the group were apprehensive about speaking out in the seminar so the spotlight was focused on me and I ended up getting some pretty nasty criticism. I can still remember the physical sensation I experienced which was like a knife being twisted in my stomach. It took nearly a day for this sensation to pass and at one stage during that time I started to have weird thoughts and was afraid that I was going crazy. The incident certainly taught me about the potentially devastating effects of criticism and I have been very careful about giving criticism, or leaving myself open to it, ever since.

Important factors involved in determining the impact of criticism are the intention of the person giving it and whether it comes with constructive suggestions for change. If the intention of the criticisor is to do anything other than be helpful then the criticism is likely to be destructive. Even if the criticisor is attempting to be helpful but no ideas are given about how the person can change their behaviour its effect may well be more often destructive than helpful. The times when I have found criticism to be most helpful have been those when it was accompanied with specific suggestions about what or how I could change.

Holland and Ward (1990) have described a model which is useful in considering how to respond to criticism. The four steps of the model are described below.

### 7.8.1 Step 1: Listening to the criticism

Listening skills are useful in clarifying the criticism. Open questions such as, 'How do you mean?' or 'Can you be more specific?' are helpful in finding out exactly what the criticism is aimed at. You may also want to ask whether there are any other criticisms the person has. If there are others then you may as well find out about them. If there aren't any others then at least you know this. Also, asking for more criticism suggests to the criticisor that you are listening and are open to feedback. When the other person comes up with several criticisms you need to sort out priorities and deal with them one at a time. You could say, 'It seems you are unhappy about several things, which is the most important of these?'

### 7.8.2 Step 2: Deciding on the truth

Before we respond to the criticism we should consider its validity. It may be completely true, partly true or completely untrue. The main difficulty is in putting your feelings 'on hold' while you decide which it is! Criticism typically has an immediate emotional 'dampening' effect on people and it is very difficult to make an objective decision in these circumstances. Also, some people are so lacking in confidence they accept all criticism of themselves, while others refuse to accept the validity of any criticism because of the pain it would cause them. Given these difficulties it is not easy to decide on the degree of truth in any criticism one receives but it is important to attempt to do so.

### 7.8.3 Step 3: Responding assertively

If we consider the criticism to be completely true then it is best to agree with the criticisor, make a brief apology and assure them you will correct the situation. For example, 'I'm sorry about not consulting you on this matter. I'll make sure it doesn't happen again'.

If we consider the criticism is partly true then we should agree with the part considered to be valid, briefly apologize, and at the same time correct the part which is false. For example, 'Yes, I did make a mistake in that case and I regret that, but I don't accept that I'm making mistakes all the time these days. I make occasional errors like anyone else'.

If we consider the criticism to be completely false then we should clearly reject it, tell the other person exactly how the criticism makes us feel, ask for an explanation of their comments and make an affirmative statement about ourselves. For example, 'I don't agree that I was wrong in that case and am greatly offended by the suggestion. What grounds could you possibly have for making such a comment? I believe my relationships with clients are excellent'.

### 7.8.4 Step 4: Letting go

It is important not to dwell on any criticism you receive. Decide to use what you have learned from the criticism and about the criticisor and move on. I know this is 'much easier said than done' but we mustn't let ourselves be deflected from our goals by what is, after all, just one person's opinion.

### 7.9 RESPONDING TO COMPLIMENTS

Unlike criticism, compliments are very unlikely to be harmful yet many people find them difficult to accept. There are several possible reasons for this. Most people are brought up to believe that it is immodest to boast or even to talk positively about themselves. Others are simply embarrassed to be the focus of attention, while those with low self-esteem believe that they do not deserve the compliments anyway. Many people believe that a person who gives compliments is insincere and must really want something.

For these reasons many people tend to discount compliments by either looking embarrassed, changing the subject, giving credit to someone else or giving a compliment in return. Comments used to discount compliments include: 'It was nothing really', 'Anyone could have done it', 'It looks better than it really is', 'What, this old thing?', and 'You could have done better.' This is very unfortunate because the discounting of compliments acts as a mild punishment to people giving them which makes them reluctant to give compliments in the future. The impact on the person doing the discounting is more serious since eventually other people will no longer give them any positive feedback.

Given the above discussion, it is clearly important for people to learn to accept compliments graciously. One way of doing this is simply to respond positively, with a thank you. For example, 'Thank you. I appreciate that' or, 'Thank you, I'm pleased you think so.' Another way of responding is with a comment. For example, 'Thank you, I enjoyed doing it' or, 'Thank you. It's one of my favourites.' If you are in any doubt about the sincerity of the compliment then you can check this out by adding a clarifying question. For example, 'Thank you, Tom. What was it in particular you liked about my presentation?' or 'Thank you, Mary. What was it about the report that interested you.'

## 7.10 GIVING COMPLIMENTS

Professionals who work with children with disabilities are well aware of the value of giving positive reinforcement or complimentary feedback to these children. However, there is often a great reluctance to apply this same principle to their parents and to colleagues. Complimenting adults on doing a good job provides invaluable feedback and seldom goes unappreciated. The importance of complimenting people was brought home to me several years ago in Australia. I was on a bus doing the three-day trip from Perth to Sydney, when seemingly in the middle of nowhere, the bus stopped and this huge, dishevelled, elderly man got on the bus and came and sat next to me. My initial apprehension soon faded when we began to talk and he turned out to be one of the most interesting people I have ever met. As the journey passed he told me his life story and showed me his bag of half a dozen large opals which were his only valuable possessions. He came across as a very wise and mature person who knew of and accepted his place in the wider scheme of things. After we had got to know each other fairly well he told me his 'secret' of how he managed to get on with everyone. He would find something he genuinely liked or admired about people and would make a point of telling them about it. He had developed this technique when he was forced to work with someone who was very aversive and he was so impressed with its success he had used it ever since. As he got up to get off the bus he turned to me and said, 'Well, I have done a lot of talking. You must be a very good listener.' He had used his 'secret' technique on me. How I wish I had accepted this feedback graciously, or even managed to tell him what an interesting person he was to listen to. But, I'm ashamed to admit, I discounted the compliment with a modest, 'Oh, no, no.'

In giving compliments it is important to be genuine. For instance giving compliments to try to cheer people up or to flatter them generally doesn't work. It is better to be honest, because if you are not sincere about the compliment then the other person is likely to sense this from your body language. Compliments should be given directly to the person involved rather than to a third person. It is somehow easier to tell a third person the positive feedback but this indirect approach is not as effective as being assertive and giving the feedback directly to the person. The content of the compliment should be specific and tell the person exactly what you appreciate about them or like about what they have done. For example, 'Your session with those parents yesterday was excellent. I think it helped them a great deal.'

Bolton (1979) suggests that giving compliments is a way of letting people know what it is about them that you value, thereby enhancing the relationship. This 'descriptive recognition' has three steps. First, you tell the other person the specific behaviour which you value. Then, you tell him or her how what they have done has made you feel. Finally, you mention the positive effect of the other's behaviour on your life. Bolton suggests using the formula, 'When you . . . I feel . . . because . . .' in order to learn how to give descriptive recognition, in the same way that the 'You feel . . . because' formula is used to learn reflection of feelings. Once you feel confident with it the formula can be dropped and it made more natural. Some examples of descriptive recognition are: 'When you co-lead the group with me I feel much more confident because I know I have your support' or 'When you took over that case for me yesterday I was relieved and very grateful because it enabled me to deal properly with the emergency we had.'

## 7.11 EXPRESSING FEELINGS

An important function of professionals is to help parents with children with disabilities to express their feelings appropriately. As explained in Chapter 2, parents typically experience intense feelings in coming to terms with the disability. They also tend to experience intense feelings associated with the demands of caring for their children, which are often related to the frustrations involved in obtaining suitable educational and recreational services. However, many societies do not encourage the expression of feelings so people tend to suppress them. This passive method of coping with our emotions works reasonably well until feelings get too intense and burst out in the form of an aggressive response. So when we do express emotion at such times it is done in such a way that it is likely to bring a negative reaction from other people. Through this kind of conditioning we have learned inappropriate ways of communicating feelings and come to expect a negative reaction whenever we do so. What we need to learn are assertive ways of expressing emotion which enable us to communicate feelings without violating the rights of others.

Gordon (1970) made a useful contribution to improving this situation when he proposed using 'I' messages to express feelings. The simplest form of 'I' message includes the words '*I feel*'. For example, 'When you do that I feel angry.' This is preferred to, 'You make me angry when you do that.' which is a 'You' message. The 'You' message communicates to the other person that you are blaming them for your feelings, so this tends to make them react defensively. Whereas, with 'I' messages you take responsibility for your own feelings. 'I' messages therefore enable you to express your feelings directly to another person without getting a negative reaction from them. In fact 'I' messages tend to facilitate empathic responses from the other person. On the other hand they can leave you vulnerable to a 'put down' if the other person has the kind of aversive personality discussed above, so 'I' messages must be used with care in this situation.

There are several more complex forms of 'I' messages. First, there is the formula, *'I feel . . . because . . .'* which is used to communicate both the feelings and the reason for the feelings. For example, 'I feel annoyed because I didn't get your support in the meeting.' Second, an even more complex form of 'I' message is the formula, *'I feel . . . because . . . I think that . . .'*. This is used to communicate the feelings, the reasons for the feelings and the irrational thoughts which are associated with them. For example, 'I feel angry because, when you contradict me, it makes me think you have no confidence in my judgement.'

Since, when we express our feelings it somehow makes us clearer about what we want, it makes sense to link 'I' messages to the expression of our desires. Formulae for doing this are, *'I feel . . . and I'd like . . .'* and at a higher muscle level, *'I feel . . . and I want . . .'*. For example, 'I feel annoyed that I've had to bring this back and I'd like it fixed properly this time' and, 'I feel frustrated with the situation and I want it sorted out.' Of course, it is not essential to express your feelings in order to state the needs which are based on these feelings. Different muscle levels of the formula, *'I want . . .'* can be used to do this. For example, 'I would like the job finished today' or 'I want the job finished today' or 'I demand that the job is finished today.'

It is not by chance that most of the examples of the use of 'I' messages above involve the expression of anger. It is certainly the most problematic emotion for most people to express. This is partly because there are usually more societal sanctions on anger than other emotions and also because anger is difficult to express assertively. The following are guidelines which specifically focus on the expression of anger. However, they can be used to facilitate the assertive expression of any emotion.

1.  Recognize that anger is a natural, healthy, non-evil feeling.
2.  Remember you are responsible for your own feelings.
3.  Remember that anger can be expressed assertively rather than aggressively.

4. Learn to recognize the things that trigger your anger.
5. Realise that feeling angry does not make you right.
6. Remember that people don't have to change just because you're angry.
7. Learn to relax and apply this when you're angry.
8. Deal with issues spontaneously when they arise. Don't stew.
9. Develop assertive methods for expressing your anger.
10. Use appropriate muscle levels for expressing anger.

### 7.12 GIVING CONSTRUCTIVE FEEDBACK

Giving constructive feedback to others is an important skill for both our professional and personal lives. Whereas criticism is mostly given without the intention of helping the other person, constructive feedback is often aimed at helping them to function better, although this need not always be the case. A model for providing constructive feedback which I have found extremely useful is one that I adapted from the DESC script popularized by Bower and Bower (1976). DESC stands for: describe; express; specify; and, consequences. This is a technique which professionals find valuable in giving feedback to parents of children with disabilities and also to their colleagues and which, in addition, parents find extremely useful in handling difficulties with professionals. The four steps involved in using the modified DESC scripts are described below.

### 7.12.1 Describe

First of all you describe the behaviour of concern in the most specific and objective terms possible. For example, 'When you change treatment procedures without consulting me ...'

### 7.12.2 Express or explain

Then you either express your feelings about this behaviour or explain the difficulties it causes for you, or sometimes usefully include both in your statement. Your explanation or your feelings should be expressed calmly and positively without blaming or judging the other person, or 'putting them down.' For example, ' . . . I get very annoyed (*express*) because parents may become confused and even lose confidence in us' (*explain*).

### 7.12.3 Specify

Then you specify the exact change in behaviour you want from the other person. Only one change is suggested and the size of the change is such that it is well within the other person's capability to make the change. For example, ' . . . So, in future, will you make sure you consult me before making such decisions . . .?'

### 7.12.4 Consequences

The consequences which are likely to result from the other person complying with our request for the change in behaviour are stated. The benefits for the both of you should be stated first along with any concessions which you are prepared to make. For example, ' . . . Then, we will be able to maintain our excellent working relationship and parents will be clear about our treatment plans.'

If the other person is not willing to comply then the modified DESC script should be repeated at progressively higher muscle levels, with the highest muscle level including the negative consequences for the person of not complying with the request. For example, ' . . . If you do not consult me as I suggest then I will have to insist on all your treatment plans being formally submitted to me for approval.'

### 7.12.5 Preparation and delivery

Although the modified DESC script is simple enough to be thought up and delivered on the spot it is usually best to write it out beforehand. This gives you the opportunity of making sure the wording is the most appropriate and the chance to rehearse it with a third person if you are uncertain about it. You then need to decide when, where and how you are going to deliver it. In fact, the modified DESC script is best delivered as part of the six part assertion process described at the end of this chapter.

### 7.13 COLLABORATIVE PROBLEM-SOLVING

Often professionals working with children with disabilities find that their opinions differ from those of parents or their colleagues. This can lead to a deterioration in relationships unless these difficulties are resolved. Bolton (1979) has proposed a model for collaboration in solving problems which has been found to be useful in this situation. The six steps of the model are described below.

### 7.13.1 Define problem in terms of needs of each person

This involves the use of active listening in order to clarify the other person's needs and, if possible, to understand the reason for these needs. It also involves stating your own needs assertively. This is a key element of the model and may take up half of the total time required for the process.

### 7.13.2 Brainstorm possible solutions

Once both persons' needs are understood brainstorming can be used to seek solutions which meet both sets of needs. First, as many potential solutions as possible should be listed, without attempting to evaluate or clarify any of them. Wild ideas should be included as these often spark off more creative solutions. Then you should attempt to clarify and expand on each other's ideas.

### 7.13.3 Select solutions which meet both parties' needs

You then choose, from the list of potential solutions, the one which best meets the needs of both parties. This will probably involve discussing the relative merits of several solutions in meeting each other's needs.

### 7.13.4 Plan who will do what, where and by when

It may be useful to make a written note of the decision about what each party will do, where it will be done and when it will be completed by.

### 7.13.5 Implement the plan

It is clearly important that each party should attempt to follow the agreement closely in implementing the plan.

### 7.13.6 Evaluate the process and the solution

An essential part of the problem-solving process is to agree a time when both parties can meet to evaluate how well the solution is meeting each of their needs.

### 7.14. A SIX-STEP MODEL FOR ASSERTION

Now that a comprehensive set of assertion skills have been discussed we can consider a model for using assertion strategies in a wide range of situations. The model presented here has been adapted from that proposed by Bolton (1979). The model requires alternation between the skills of assertion and those of active listening, which were covered in Chapter 5. It is a model which professionals who work with parents of children with disabilities will find helpful to keep in their heads along with the counselling model described in Chapter 6. The six steps of the assertion model are described below.

### 7.14.1 Preparation

The first stage of the process is to prepare for delivering the assertion message. It is usually best to write out the actual words you intend to use in the message. The DESC script, discussed above, can be adapted to form the basis of assertion messages to fit most situations. Once the assertion message is written you can consider its appropriateness. You need to ask yourself whether the message respects the rights of the other person and whether you have sufficient rapport with him or her to deliver such a message. You also need to ask yourself if the concern is important enough to justify the trouble you are going to. Finally, you need to consider the likelihood of your message achieving its goal. If there is not a good chance of this happening you need to re-consider the wisdom of going ahead with it. This is particularly true when you are first learning to be more assertive. You don't want to start with a failure, you need a situation in which there is a good chance of success.

If after considering all this you still decide to go ahead with the message then you should rehearse it. Ideally this should be done with another person who can give you feedback on it and perhaps help you improve on the wording. If this is not possible then rehearsing in front of a mirror can be helpful. But for most situations simply reading it out to yourself is quite sufficient. You should then decide on the best time and place to deliver your request. Remember that, as noted earlier in this chapter, people are more likely to agree to requests at certain times such as, when they are relaxed, when they are in a good mood and after they have eaten. It is usually better if you can deliver the assertion message to the other person in private and in a place where you are not likely to be interrupted.

### 7.14.2 Delivering the assertion message

It is best to begin with a brief friendly preface, perhaps thanking the person for setting aside time to see you. Then go straight into the message, making sure that you are using the physical and vocal assertive skills discussed earlier in this chapter.

### 7.14.3 Using silence

When you have delivered the message it is important to leave a silence to give the other person time to think and to express any reservations they may have. Silence is also useful in encouraging the other person to keep talking rather than withdraw from the interaction which is a response some people attempt to use when someone is being assertive with them.

### 7.14.4 Actively listening

Listening skills are used to deal with any defensiveness encountered from the other person. Active listening helps to clarify the person's point of view and to explore what, if anything, is really bothering them about your message.

By using active listening you are also able to defuse hostile responses, to side-step questions and debates and to cope with emotional responses such as the other person beginning to cry.

### 7.14.5 Recycling the process

When you have listened and the other person has had the opportunity to express his or her views, you then restate the DESC script, or other assertion message, at a slightly higher muscle level. You again leave a silence and actively listen to the person's reactions. You then repeat the process once more, again at a slightly higher muscle level. You go on repeating the process, alternating between assertion and listening responses, until the other person accepts your message.

### 7.14.6 Agreeing a solution

At the conclusion of the meeting the other person should have accepted the change in behaviour specified in your DESC script or come up with an alternative solution which meets your needs. If this hasn't happened then you will need to use the collaborative problem-solving process discussed above in order for you to come up with a solution acceptable to you both. It isn't necessary for the other person to like the final solution, just to agree to it. You should paraphrase the agreed solution to ensure both parties have the same understanding. You should then thank the other person for their time and arrange for another meeting so that you can both check that the solution is working.

### 7.15 SUMMARY

This chapter has addressed the wide range of assertion skills which professionals working with parents of children with disabilities can make use of in their dealings with parents and with their colleagues. Assertive behaviour is distinguished from passive, indirect and aggressive responses. Assertive rights and basic elements of assertiveness are discussed. Assertive skills covered include: making and refusing requests;

coping with criticism and aggression; giving constructive feedback, expressing feelings; collaborative problem solving; and, giving and receiving compliments. Finally, a six-step model for using assertion skills is presented.

Another set of skills which professionals working in this field need are the skills involved in effectively leading groups of various kinds. These skills are discussed in the following chapter.

# 8

# Groupwork skills

## 8.1 VALUE OF GROUPWORK WITH PARENTS

In earlier chapters of this book I have made the point that parents of children with disabilities have specialized counselling and guidance needs. Counselling is mainly needed in order to facilitate the parents' adaptation to the disability and address any concerns they may have. Guidance is mainly needed in order to help parents cope with the learning and behavioural difficulties which their children present. Typically, professionals attempt to meet these needs through the provision of services to individual parents and families. Group counselling and group guidance are less often available to parents. Some parents feel more at ease with individual counselling or guidance but most parents benefit from participation in group sessions. There are, in fact, some important advantages of working with groups of parents.

### 8.1.1 Advantages over individual counselling

One advantage of group counselling over individual sessions is that, in talking with others, parents realize that they are not the only ones with problems. This sharing of common problems typically facilitates the experience of feeling that they are 'in the same boat' which is thought to help parents feel less isolated. This effect has been termed 'universality' by Yalom (1985) and is considered to be a particularly therapeutic component of group counselling. In addition, parents can express their feelings regarding their children with disabilities and discover that others experience similar emotions. Realizing that other parents have similar feelings is considered to help parents come to terms with their own. For example, some parents experience a lot of guilt related to having thought about getting rid of their disabled child in some way or other, so it is a tremendous relief to them to find out that many other parents have had similar thoughts. Further, in a group with other parents of children with disabilities, it is often easier for parents to reveal concerns which they have not felt able to bring up in individual counselling sessions with a professional (Kroth, 1985).

Another advantage of group counselling is that parents experience mutual support from the other group members which helps them to become more confident in their own ability as parents. The group also provides several models for, and the opportunity to practice, the expression of feelings and the ability to listen empathically to others. The group therefore provides a setting in which parents can learn to improve communication skills (Dinkmeyer and Muro, 1979). Finally, the group process itself involves several factors, in addition to those noted above, which promote personal growth among group members. These have been termed 'curative factors' by Yalom (1985) and include group cohesiveness, altruism and the instillation of hope. I have often found it remarkable to see just how much parents have gained in confidence and self-esteem over the course of some group work they have been involved in. In fact, I have become convinced that bringing parents together in a group with other parents of children with similar disabilities, and facilitating their interaction, is one of the most useful things professionals can do for them.

## 8.1.2 Advantages over individual guidance

Most parents of children with disabilities want to receive guidance from professionals in order to help them cope with their children's behaviour problems and facilitate their children's development. This guidance is usually provided on a one-to-one basis, by professionals working with individual parents or families. However, such guidance can also be provided by professionals working with groups of parents, such as in behavioural group training (Hornby and Singh, 1983). In fact, there are several advantages of providing guidance to a group of parents as compared to working with individual parents or families. One of the major benefits of group guidance is that when parents participate in a group they learn together in a mutually supportive atmosphere. They are often more responsive to changing their opinions and learning new strategies in this situation (Kroth, 1985). Also, in a group, parents are exposed to a wider range of behaviour problems and learning difficulties, and the procedures used to deal with them, than they would experience in individual guidance sessions. This should facilitate their handling of problems encountered in the future.

Another advantage is that, in a group, solutions for a particular parent's difficulties will be suggested by other parents who may have experienced similar difficulties in the past. Parents are almost always responsive to such potential solutions. The group also provides numerous possibilities for modelling and role play of difficult situations and of procedures to deal with them. In addition, the group is a source of ideas for potential reinforcers, of motivation for parents to implement suggested treatment procedures, and of social reinforcement for parents' achievements (Rose, 1977).

## 8.1.3 Advantages to professionals

There are also advantages of working with groups of parents, over individual work, for the professionals involved. Obviously, since more parents can be reached in a group than individually it is possible to provide guidance or counselling to a greater number of parents than could be managed using an individual approach. Also, there are times when several parents are experiencing the same difficulty and professionals can provide guidance to them all at the same time rather than individually, thereby using their time more efficiently. This is, in fact the way that I first became involved in group work. When working as an educational psychologist I noticed that there were six referrals from parents, whose children attended the same large primary school, all wanting guidance on managing their children's behaviour. I decided to see them in a group mainly to save time, but as the sessions progressed I became more and more convinced of the value of the group approach.

Another advantage is that, because of the efficient use of time, it is possible to justify two or more professionals working together with the group of parents and thereby sharing skills and knowledge with each other. Working with colleagues such as psychologists, speech therapists, occupational therapists and social workers in groups has contributed significantly to my expertise in working with parents. In addition, the parents in the group are a source of knowledge and skills which professionals can utilize. I have certainly found that working with parent groups has educated me about parents' experiences and needs.

### 8.1.4 Disadvantages of working with groups of parents

There are, of course, some negative aspects of doing group work with parents of children with disabilities. First, not all parents feel comfortable being in a group with other parents. Some prefer to be seen individually. Therefore professionals can't reach all parents this way, which means that group experiences need to be provided in addition to individual services, which can add to professional workloads. Second, in order to obtain maximum participation in group work with parents of children with disabilities, it is often necessary to hold sessions in evenings or at the weekend, which can cut into professionals' leisure time. Third, working with groups of parents requires skills and knowledge over and above that needed for individual work.

### 8.2 PARENT WORKSHOPS

Group work with parents of children with disabilities has generally taken the form of either reflective counselling or behavioural training. In reflective group counselling the focus is on the parents' emotional needs. Parents are encouraged to express, and attempt to resolve, their concerns and feelings and thereby improve in their adaptation to their child with a disability (Hornby and Singh, 1982). In behavioural group training the focus is on changing the children's behaviour. Parents are taught behaviour modification techniques in order to improve the management of their children's behavioural and learning difficulties (Hornby and Singh, 1983).

In a study which compared the effectiveness of these two approaches with parents of children with disabilities, Tavormina (1975) reported positive outcomes for both reflective and behavioural groups. In a further study it was found that a combination of reflective and behavioural approaches was the most effective (Tavormina, Hampson and Luscomb, 1976). Positive outcomes have also been reported when aspects of the reflective and behavioural approaches have been combined in other workshops for parents of children with disabilities (Attwood, 1978, 1979; Cunningham and Jeffree, 1975).

Based on these reports a model for a parent workshop which combines reflective counselling with behavioural training was developed by the author and his colleagues in New Zealand. The aim of this work was to develop a type of parent workshop which combines group guidance with group counselling in order to provide a supportive environment in which parents can learn new skills and gain confidence through talking with other parents. The workshop has been used with several groups of parents of mentally handicapped children and also separately for parents of children with hearing impairment and those with physical disabilities (Hornby and Murray, 1983).

## 8.3 ORGANIZATION OF WORKSHOPS

The structure and organization of the workshop model has evolved into the form presented here, from changes made to the original organization, based on feedback received from parents and professionals. A summary of the main aspects of workshop organization is presented below.

### 8.3.1 **Venue and recruitment**

Recruitment of parents for the workshops has generally been carried out by sending a letter of invitation to all parents of children attending the relevant facilities, such as special schools or pre-school programmes for children with disabilities.

### 8.3.2 **Sessions**

Between six and eight weekly two-hour evening sessions have been found to be the most satisfactory. Less than six sessions is too few to present the relevant material and to benefit from the therapeutic process which the group of parents experience as the workshop progresses. More than eight sessions is too great a commitment of time and too tiring for parents and professionals alike. Anything greater than a one week break between sessions, such as fortnightly or monthly sessions, has led to a considerable drop in attendance in past workshops and is therefore avoided. Evening sessions are generally easier for both professionals and parents to attend. Two hours has been found to be the optimum time for the length of sessions. Any less leaves insufficient time for both discussion and lecture presentation.

### 8.3.3 **Number of parents**

A reasonably large number of parents can be catered for by taking the group of parents as a whole during the lecture presentations and final summary sections of the workshop and dividing them into small groups during the discussion section. The size of the small groups need to be large enough to give a reasonable range of children and problems but small enough to provide sufficient time for each parent to discuss his or her concern. From six to ten parents has been found the most satisfactory size for the small groups.

### 8.3.4 **Group leaders**

Small group discussions are led by professionals with previous experience of leading such groups. Groups often include a less experienced co-leader who works in tandem with the leader. In this way co-leaders can be trained to lead their own groups in subsequent parent workshops.

## 8.4 FORMAT OF WORKSHOPS

The format for the parent workshops which has been found the most useful is summarized in Fig. 8.1. The sessions are typically divided into four parts: socializing; lecture presentation; small group discussion; and, summary, handouts and homework.

### 8.4.1 Socializing

The first fifteen minutes of the workshops is used to help parents relax since many parents experience anxiety when they first come along to group sessions where they are expected to talk about their children. It provides an opportunity for parents to get to know other parents and professionals informally and also overcomes the problem of late arrivals interrupting the lecture presentations.

### 8.4.2 Lecture presentation

Lectures of approximately 20 minutes in length are presented to the whole group of parents who are usually seated in a horseshoe arrangement around the speaker. The first lecture typically consists of an outline of the workshop and a brief

---

7.30–7.45 p.m.  *Socializing*. Tea and coffee are served while parents talk informally with professionals and each other.

7.45–8.05 p.m.  *Lecture presentation*. A 20-minute lecture on a topic of concern to the parents is presented by the appropriate professional.

8.05–9.15 p.m.  *Small group discussion*. Parents are divided into small groups in order to participate in discussion. Opportunity is provided for discussion of the applications of the lecture content to specific problems brought forward by parents. Parents are encouraged to express and explore any problems, concerns or feelings regarding their disabled children.

9.15–9.30 p.m.  *Summary, handouts and homework*. The large group is re-formed so that issues raised in small group discussions can be summarized and shared, homework tasks explained and handouts summarizing the content of lectures distributed.

---

**Figure 8.1** Format of parent workshops.

introduction to the principles of behaviour modification. At the end of the first session parents are asked to fill out a sheet in order to indicate their choice of lectures for the following sessions. Lecture topics depend on the types of disability and the ages of the children whose parents are involved in the workshops. Topics have included: speech and language development; behaviour management; social and emotional development; sexual development; services available; recreational activities; and, vocational placement.

### 8.4.3 Small group discussion

The largest block of time in the workshop, of approximately 70 minutes, is given over to discussion which is conducted in small groups. Discussions are conducted in separate rooms, with chairs arranged in a circle. Groups typically consist of a leader, a co-leader and six to ten parents. Leaders guide the discussions using a combination of reflective and behavioural skills. The reflective and behavioural skills used, and how they are combined, are discussed in the following section.

Co-leaders work in tandem with leaders by focusing on the group dynamics and on the body language of group members so that they can draw the leader's attention to a parent who may want to say something but hasn't been noticed. All leaders and co-leaders meet for half an hour before each session to plan the session and for a short time afterwards in order to debrief and discuss the subsequent sessions.

Problems and concerns brought forward by parents in each of the workshops organized to date have ranged over a wide area. They have included:

- concern about what happens to child when parents get older;
- difficulty in coping with temper tantrums;
- dealing with inappropriate sexual behaviour;
- coping with sleeping problems;
- dealing with toileting problems;
- the need for parents to have a break from the child;
- coping with adults who stare and children who tease;
- finding suitable leisure activities;
- sorting out the best educational placement for the child;

- coping with children's communication difficulties;
- the difficulty of encouraging independence rather than doing things for their children.

### 8.4.4 Summary, handouts and homework

With all the parents present a leader or co-leader from each small group reports back on the issues and concerns discussed. Homework tasks, such as the completion of behaviour observation forms, are explained and the forms distributed along with a summary of the lecture content for that session.

A point is made of concluding the formal aspects of each session punctually since many parents will have arranged baby-sitters and need to be home promptly. However, it has been found that some parents will remain to talk with other parents or professionals for up to half an hour afterwards.

## 8.5 SKILLS USED BY GROUP LEADERS

### 8.5.1 Combination of reflective and behavioural approaches

As was stated above, the leaders guide the small group discussions using a combination of reflective and behavioural skills. Reflective skills are used in order to facilitate open but guided discussion of parents' concerns, problems and feelings. Behavioural skills are employed in order to teach parents how to apply behavioural principles to the learning and management difficulties which their children present.

The reflective and behavioural approaches are combined using the counselling model described in Chapter 6 as a framework. In this model the professional begins by using reflective skills in order to encourage parents to openly discuss their problems, concerns and feelings. Once the problems of greatest concern have been identified and clarified the professional begins to introduce behavioural skills in order to help parents work towards finding solutions to their problems. This progression from a reflective to a behavioural approach is paralleled by the way the small group discussions are led. Parents are invited to discuss whatever problems or concerns they choose. At first, reflective skills are used in order to facilitate and guide the discussion. Later, behavioural skills are used in order to help parents find solutions to their problems.

Different amounts of time are spent using the reflective approach depending on the nature of the concern or problem. For some problems brought forward by parents, such as bed-wetting, the leaders would move quickly on to the behavioural approach, since this is clearly a practical problem. For other concerns, such as about adults who stare at children with disabilities when they are taken out, more time will need to be spent using reflective skills before moving on to behavioural skills, because parents will have feelings they need to express about this situation before going on to decide what to do about it in the future. Finally, for occasions when parents are experiencing strong emotions, such as about how they were told of the child's disability, reflective skills alone may be sufficient, since the parents' main need is likely to be to express their feelings about the way it was done. The progression from the reflective to the behavioural approach is illustrated by the flow diagram presented in Fig. 8.2. The three arrows going into the behavioural approach are intended to illustrate the three points at which leaders would begin to use behavioural

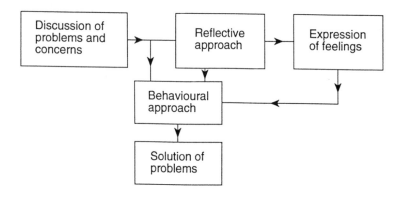

**Figure 8.2** Model for progression from reflective to behavioural approach.

skills in the examples cited above. The reflective and behavioural skills used by group leaders are described below.

### 8.5.2 Reflective skills

#### (a) Reflection

The active listening skills described in Chapter 5 are used in order to help parents explore their concerns and feelings. At the beginning of the discussions the emphasis is usually on paraphrasing or reflecting the content of parents' statements. That is, the key points in what parents are saying are re-stated back to them for clarification and to encourage self-exploration. As parents begin to open up and explore their concerns both content and feelings are reflected. For example, 'Your main problem is coping with her tantrums and this makes you feel pretty helpless.'

#### (b) Universalizing

Once a problem or concern, and the parent's feelings about it, have been expressed and clarified, leaders ask whether any other members of the group have been in a similar situation. This is done in order to help parents become aware that their concerns and feelings are shared by others and thereby generate a feeling of being 'in the same boat' which, as noted earlier in this chapter, has a therapeutic effect on parents. The leader would ask, 'Has anyone else experienced this?'

#### (c) Linking

Leaders point out common themes expressed but not recognized as such by different parents. This helps parents listen to one another and gain a greater understanding of what they are experiencing. For example, 'Michelle, this sounds the same sort of problem that Linda talked of earlier.'

#### (d) Self-disclosure

Where relevant, leaders tell of their own difficulties and feelings from their experiences in their professional roles or as parents themselves. For example, 'I, too, find it difficult to discuss sex openly and without embarrassment.' As noted in Chapter 6, such self-disclosure is important in communicating genuineness, that is, letting parents know that the leaders have their problems too. This is important in establishing the rapport and trust necessary for parents to open up and disclose the things that worry them most.

### (e) Summarizing

The leaders summarize at various points in order to help parents see the wider picture and to keep the discussion moving forward productively. Summarizing can also be used to draw the discussion to a conclusion while at the same time emphasizing what has been learned. For example, 'We have talked about ... and ... and we seem to agree that ...'.

### (f) Structuring

The leaders guide the discussion by re-directing parents when they wander off the topic or are monopolizing the discussion. For example, 'Could we take up the point that Heather raised?' Of course, in any group some participants will say more than others, but if it is clear that a parent is dominating the discussion to the extent that other parents are not able to air their concerns then the leaders need to intervene. Usually this can be done with the kind of verbal structuring noted above, using progressively higher muscle levels, as suggested in Chapter 7. Very occasionally, this will not be enough and a quiet word will need to be had with a particularly domineering parent at the end of the session. On the one occasion that I can remember this happening, the parent concerned came to the group leader at the end of the workshop and thanked her for helping him limit his input, because as he explained, he usually talked far too much!

### 8.5.3 Behavioural skills

### (a) Informing

At appropriate points in the discussions, leaders provide information from their professional expertise or point out the applicability of techniques presented in lectures to the problems brought forward by parents.

### (b) Questioning

When parents talk of specific difficulties with their disabled children leaders ask questions in order to establish the antecedents, the behaviour of concern and the consequences for the child. This helps to clarify the problem situation and to teach parents to apply the principles of behaviour modification to difficulties encountered with their children. For example,

'What exactly did he do?'
'What led up to it?'
'What did you do about it?'
'What happened then?'

### (c) Problem solving

The leaders encourage the group to suggest techniques to deal with the problem behaviours of concern to each parent. The techniques of brainstorming and evaluating options, which were discussed in Chapter 6, are used to help parents decide on a plan of action to deal with their particular problems.

### (d) Behavioural rehearsal

When necessary, leaders model behaviour modification techniques and get parents to role-play these within the group before trying them at home.

### (e) Task setting

Parents are asked to implement the techniques and action plans selected over the week between sessions and report back to the group at the next session.

### (f) Feedback

The leaders provide feedback on parents' progress with the problem situations they have chosen to deal with at appropriate points during discussions.

## (g) Homework

At the end of some sessions parents are given tasks to complete at home and bring to the next session. For example, it is often useful to ask parents to fill out a developmental checklist or observation record on their children.

## 8.6 EVALUATION OF PARENT WORKSHOPS

Some parent workshops in which the author has been involved have been subject to rigorous evaluation (Hornby, 1992b; Hornby and Singh, 1984). These research studies have provided evidence that parents improve in their ability to apply various techniques to their children following attending a parent workshop. However, it is usually only considered necessary to include three simple forms of evaluation: an attendance record; a post-workshop questionnaire; and, clinical evaluation by the group leaders.

### 8.6.1 Attendance

A record should be kept of the attendance of parents at each session. Then, at the end of the workshop a percentage figure of the overall attendance of parents can be obtained. Attwood (1978) has claimed that an attendance record provides the most objective assessment of the benefit of such a workshop to the parents since parents are seen as 'voting with their feet' about the value of the workshops. Overall attendance rates for the parent workshops conducted by the author up to this time range from 70 to 90%, which is considered satisfactory.

### 8.6.2 Post-workshop questionnaire

At the end of the final session of each workshop parents are asked to complete a questionnaire concerning its benefits and limitations. The importance of assessing consumer satisfaction in this way has been stressed by various authors (Forehand, Wells and Griest, 1980; Tavormina, Hampson and Luscomb, 1976).

Parents' responses on the post-workshop questionnaires used in the various workshops which I have led have shown considerable similarity. The vast majority of parents report feeling more confidence in their ability to parent their child with a disability after attending the workshops. Also, most parents comment that they greatly appreciate the opportunity to share problems and feelings with other parents who are 'in the same boat' as them. Many parents comment on the increased knowledge which they have gained from attending the workshop. Negative feedback from parents is typically related to the desire for more time for both discussion and for lecture presentations.

### 8.6.3 Clinical impressions

Discussions among the professionals following workshops are useful in evaluating their effectiveness. Professionals typically consider that a major positive feature of the workshops is the facilitation of interactions between parents of children with similar disabilities. Parents are observed to gain a great deal of support and confidence from sharing their problems, concerns and feelings with others in similar situations. Professionals typically comment on the caring atmosphere and cohesiveness which develops in the small groups. This is usually evidenced during the final session of the workshop when parents often exchange phone numbers and suggest further meetings of the group. Informal feedback suggests that some parents remain in contact with each other long after the parent workshops have ended.

### 8.7 WORKSHOPS FOR OTHER FAMILY MEMBERS

Workshops have also been developed in order to address the needs of other members of families who have children with disabilities. Workshops for siblings, fathers, and grandparents were developed as part of the Supporting Extended Family Members (SEFAM) project at the University of Washington in Seattle (Fewell and Vadasy, 1986).

### 8.7.1 Grandparent workshops

Workshops for grandparents were held on Saturday mornings and included either a guest speaker invited to address matters of concern to grandparents or a panel of parents or siblings to talk about their experiences. Time was also scheduled for grandparents to meet in small groups, facilitated by a member of staff, to share their concerns and feelings. The workshops therefore provided opportunities for grandparents to meet each other as well as to obtain information from professionals about their grandchildren's disabilities and guidance on how to best provide support for the family (Vadasy, Fewell and Meyer, 1986).

An outgrowth of these workshops is the Helping Grand-parent Program in which experienced grandparents are trained in order to provide support to grandparents of newly diagnosed children (Sonnek, 1986). This scheme is based on the Parent-to-Parent model which is described later in this chapter.

### 8.7.2 Fathers workshops

The Fathers Program developed by the SEFAM team also uses a workshop format, meeting every two weeks on Satur-day mornings (Meyer *et al.*, 1985). There are three components to the Fathers Program, the first two of which are similar to those in workshops for parents and grandparents. First, guest speakers provide fathers with information about their children's disabilities and services available. Second, dis-cussion groups are used to enable fathers to discuss their concerns and interests with other fathers and thereby obtain peer support. Third, fathers bring their children along to the meetings so that part of the time allocated can be used for all the fathers and children to get together and take part in group activities or individual play. The aims of this component of the Fathers Program are both to encourage fathers to interact more with their children and to provide their wives with some respite from child-care responsi-bilities.

A study conducted to evaluate the effects of the Fathers Program found that fathers who participated reported less sadness, fatigue, guilt and stress as well as greater feelings of success and satisfaction, fewer problems and better decision making abilities than did other fathers of children with disabilities.

### 8.7.3 Sibling workshops

The 'sibshops' developed as part of the SEFAM project are workshops aimed at providing siblings of children with disabilities an opoportunity to meet others in the same situation, to gain specific information on disabilities, and to learn how to handle common incidents which occur in families which have a member with a disability (Meyer, Vadasy and Fewell, 1985). Sibshops have followed a similar format to the workshops described above but have also included outings and activities aimed at providing enjoyment for the siblings themselves. In order to help the younger children open up about their worries and feelings some different activities have been included. For example, siblings are asked to write down their problems on paper which is put in a box and is later taken out and read out to everyone and discussed in the group, without identifying the writer.

### 8.8 SELF-HELP GROUPS

A major growth area in mental health services in recent years has been the proliferation of self-help groups, well known examples of which are Alcoholics Anonymous and Weight Watchers (Gitterman and Shulman, 1986). Groups for parents of children with disabilities have been no exception. In most cities around the world there are now self-help groups for parents of children with most disabilities. These range from groups in which a small number of parents get together regularly for support to others which have become national organisations such as MENCAP and the Spastics Society (in England).

Many of the therapeutic factors associated with group counselling, such as universality and group cohesion, also work to promote personal growth in self-help groups. In such groups parents develop their own personal coping strategies and increase their social support networks.

In addition to the many groups for parents there are now organizations specifically for fathers, siblings and grandparents of people with disabilities. Each of these publishes a regular newsletter (Fewell and Vadasy, 1986). One type of self-help group, which has shown rapid growth in numbers in recent years is the parent-to-parent scheme. The organization of the parent-to-parent schemes which the author has been involved in is described below.

## 8.9 PARENT-TO-PARENT SCHEMES

Parent-to-parent services were first established in the USA and have subsequently spread to Canada, Australia, New Zealand, England and Ireland (Hornby, 1988; McConkey, 1985). They are support services for parents of children with disabilities in which support is provided by a team of volunteer parents who themselves have children with disabilities. Typically, parent-to-parent services operate as a telephone contact helpline. Schemes are advertised by means of leaflets, posters or cards put on notice boards in places where parents are likely to see them, such as libraries, health centres and schools. Parents seeking contact ring the helpline telephone number and are put in touch with a support parent who has a child with a similar disability.

The parent-to-parent schemes in which the writer, and his colleagues, have been involved, have emphasized training parents in basic counselling skills (Hornby, Murray and Jones, 1987). If professionals are engaged to provide this training a parent–professional partnership can form the basis of the service. By training parents to help others, professionals are assisting the development of a support network which will meet many of the parents' needs. In this way the scheme can provide a type of assistance which is complementary to that offered by professionals themselves, while making good use of the special contribution which only people who have been through similar experiences can offer (Hatch and Hinton, 1986).

### 8.9.1 Recruiting support parents

Potential support parents are initially recruited by means of contact with existing parent organizations such as the Spastics Society or MENCAP. Typically a meeting is set up to discuss the organization of a parent-to-parent scheme and explain what is involved in completing the training course. It is explained that a maximum of 14 parents can attend each course and that if any selection has to be made it will be to ensure the greatest possible diversity of support parents. This is done so that parents will represent a wide range of disabilities, ages of children and personal circumstances. Recruiting for subsequent courses is less formal. Typically, parents hear of the scheme through professionals or other parents and ask if they can join a training course. The parent-to-parent scheme can begin operation as soon as the first training course is completed. Subsequent courses then increase the number of parents available to provide support and add to the diversity of disabilities represented.

When parents are recruited it is explained that they must attend at least seven out of eight sessions and attain an adequate level of counselling skills in order to become support parents. It is the responsibility of the course leaders to ensure that people unsuitable, for whatever reason, do not become support parents. This is important for the protection of the consumers of the service and for its credibility with professionals and parents.

### 8.9.2 The training course

The parent-to-parent training course is typically conducted in a series of eight weekly sessions of two hours each. It is usually held in the evening between 7.45 and 10 pm with the first 15 minutes of each session being used for tea, coffee and socializing in order to reduce anxieties and allow for any latecomers. Sessions are best conducted in a carpeted room with chairs arranged in a circle. The room needs to be big enough for parents to be divided up into threesomes and spread around the room for role play practice of counselling skills. Besides suitability of the room, a venue which is centrally located and known to parents, such as a local clinic or educational setting, is the most suitable.

The first two sessions of the training course focus on the sharing of parents' own experiences regarding their children with disabilities. In the first session parents introduce themselves and talk about their families, in particular the child with a disability. The stage model of adaptation to disability, which was discussed in Chapter 2, is presented in the second session in order to encourage parents to talk about their reactions to the diagnosis and explore the feelings associated with this. In the next five sessions parents are taught basic counselling skills using the three-stage model of helping discussed in Chapter 6. Emphasis is placed on the development of the active listening skills described in Chapter 5. The final session focuses on the organization of the parent-to-parent scheme, including such issues as the distribution of publicity materials and the planning of a duty roster for telephone duties.

### 8.9.3 The leaders

The professionals who lead parent-to-parent training courses need experience of leading groups, knowledge of the disabilities concerned and an ability to teach basic counselling skills to adults. Since courses are usually tutored by two leaders, it is possible for these requirements to be shared between the co-leaders. During sessions, the leaders need to provide good models of the helping skills taught and use group facilitation skills such as reflection, linking, universalizing, summarizing and structuring, which were discussed earlier in this chapter.

The teaching techniques used in the course include: mini-lectures, discussions, modelling, practice of the skills in threesomes, homework and rounds, in which all the parents in turn are asked to say what they think or feel. The specific procedures used are described in detail in the Leaders' Training Manual (Hornby, Murray and Davies, 1993).

### 8.9.4 Organization of the scheme

The detail of the organizational structure of each parent-to-parent scheme is determined by the support parents with only general guidance from the professionals. Typically, a number of parents who have completed the first training course form a steering committee in order to set up the mechanics of the scheme. In order to spread the load, and ensure involvement of as many parents as possible, committee members are encouraged to share out the various administrative tasks involved in running the service, in addition to delegating tasks to the support parents whenever possible. The major responsibilities which are divided up among committee members are finance, publicity, liaison, the telephone system and training.

Finance is usually divided between two parents, one acting as treasurer, the other as fund-raising co-ordinator. Money is required to purchase an answerphone and pay for a separate telephone line, as well as for publicity material and paying nominal expenses for the professionals who lead the training groups. Typically, service clubs such as the Lions and Telethon appeals provide most of the finance required for operating parent-to-parent schemes. Thus, fund-raising is not time consuming which frees parents to fulfil the main aim of the service – to support other parents.

One parent usually co-ordinates the printing and distribution of the publicity material advertising the service. The actual distribution is carried out by the support parents, each being assigned a geographical area to cover. Another parent is assigned to fostering and maintaining positive links with government and voluntary agencies and other support groups. Tasks such as speaking to professional or community groups are shared out among support parents. A further parent co-ordinates the ongoing training of support parents through refresher sessions (held two or three times a year) and arranges further training courses for new support parents.

Usually at least four parents take responsibility for operating the telephone contact system. One organizes a roster of support parents on duty. Another changes the parents' names and phone numbers on the answerphone. A third person keeps details of all support parents and tries to match support parents with parents seeking help (in terms of the child's disability, age and so on). A fourth parent keeps a resource file of information on such things as benefits, services and possible referral agencies so that support parents needing such information can have rapid access to it.

The schemes require minimal funding and tend to result in useful parent–professional partnerships. They can contribute significantly to the support networks which are available to parents of children with special needs. Other benefits which accrue from the schemes include the personal growth which parents typically make in completing the training course and the mutual support which develops among course members. Also, links are established between parents of children who have different disabilities which helps to break down the barriers which often exist between services for the different disability groups.

## 8.10 ADVOCACY GROUPS

A type of group training for parents which has emerged recently is programmes for training parents in advocacy skills (Schilling, 1988). The aim of advocacy training is to help parents to become advocates for their own children in order to obtain the best possible services for them and ultimately to become advocates for people with disabilities in general. Advocacy training involves gaining information about the rights of children with disabilities and about how to access the resources and services available to them. It also involves parents learning assertion skills, which was discussed in Chapter 7, so that they can overcome any lack of confidence and advocate for their children assertively rather than aggressively.

Advocacy training programmes therefore typically consist of a combination of professional input and parental sharing about available resources and how to access them, plus the teaching of assertion skills through didactic presentations, along with modelling and role play of the relevant strategies. In these ways professionals are able to pass on to parents the knowledge and skills they need, thereby empowering parents to become as effective as possible in their task of caring for their children with disabilities.

## 8.11 SUMMARY

Working with groups of parents who have children with disabilities has certain advantages over individual counselling and guidance. In this chapter several types of groups relevant to families with disabled members are described. These include self-help groups, advocacy groups and workshops for siblings, fathers and grandparents. Two group programmes are discussed at length. These are parent-to-parent schemes and parent workshops. Details of the organization of these programmes are presented plus elaboration of the skills which professionals need in order to lead them.

The next chapter focuses on the skills needed by professionals in order to empower and enable parents and act as mentors for other professionals.

# 9

---

# Enabling skills

## 9.1 VALUE OF ENABLING SKILLS

Ideally professionals working in the challenging field of childhood disability need to be enabling individuals who are able to move beyond simply helping parents to overcome the difficulties they encounter in raising their children with disabilities. They need to be able to facilitate the development of parents as people, to enable them, not only to effectively fulfil their parenting role, but also to fulfil their own personal potential to the maximum possible extent. Caring for a child with a disability can be such a demanding task that it consumes all of the parents' energies and narrows their perspective on life to the extent that many of their potential areas for fulfilment are thwarted. Professionals can have a substantial positive impact on parents' lives by helping them widen their focus and attend to their own desires and aspirations. Parents can be encouraged to see that by fulfilling more of their own potential they will increase their effectiveness in caring for their children with disabilities and in the parenting of their other children as well as in their family and work roles generally.

A simple example of the kind of enabling I have in mind involved a colleague of mine, Ray Murray, and a mother of a boy with Down's syndrome who worked as a freelance journalist. This parent seemed to be spending much of her time and energy battling with the system in order to get the best services for her child. Then Ray asked her to give the after dinner speech at a conference of professionals, with a topic of, 'The fun of parenting a child with a disability.' At the end of her hilarious and, in places, very moving speech, she thanked Ray for inviting her to speak and said what a useful exercise it had been for her to prepare the speech and focus on all the positive aspects of caring for her son. Making the speech had apparently helped this parent to broaden her perspective.

In addition to enabling parents, professionals working in the field of disability should also be willing to act as mentors for their less experienced colleagues. This is a very challenging field and one in which a tremendous amount of knowledge and skills need to be learned. By providing models of facilitating attitudes and being willing to share their knowledge and skills with colleagues, professionals can have a much greater impact on the field than would come from their own work with children with disabilities and their parents.

Professionals working in the disability field therefore need to be proficient in counselling and assertion skills but also need to go beyond this to the skills required for enthusing, encouraging and empowering others. They therefore need to be highly functioning people themselves. They need to develop the personal habits required for living life at their optimum effectiveness. They also need to be able to use and teach others the skills of stress management in order to cope with the heavy interpersonal demands experienced in this field. These aspects of personal effectiveness are discussed in the remainder of this chapter.

## 9.2 BEING AN EFFECTIVE PERSON

### 9.2.1 Key components of psychological health

In order to function effectively professionals should have high levels of the six components of psychological health suggested by Cole (1982). First, they need to have high levels of *self-esteem*. That is, they must have confidence in their abilities and focus on their strengths while accepting their weaknesses. Second, they need to have a clear set of *values* which include a philosophical or spiritual guide to their behaviour. Third, they must have good *self-control* so that they can plan courses of action, choose from a wide range of options and be flexible enough to adapt to rapidly changing circumstances. Fourth, they need to be able to accept *personal responsibility* for their actions and not seek to blame others for their mistakes. Fifth, they need to develop high levels of *competence* in the whole range of life skills including personal, interpersonal, social and vocational skills. Finally, they need to have a strong sense of *social responsibility*, a desire to contribute to the care of others.

Maslow (1962), who proposed a hierarchy of human motivating factors from physiological needs through to the need for self-actualization, found in his research, that self-actualizing people were typically involved in causes outside their own concerns. In fact, Frankl (1965) considered that the need for a meaning or purpose in our lives provides a higher level of motivation than the need to self-actualize. So it appears that having a purpose in life of wanting to be of help to others is a hallmark of psychologically healthy people.

### 9.2.2 Characteristics of fully functioning people

Carkhuff and Berenson (1967) have suggested a list of characteristics of fully functioning people who have managed to attain high levels of self-actualization. Such people:
(a) act on the basis of their integrity and are unafraid of ambiguity;
(b) regard honesty and creativity as a way of life;
(c) live life intensely and spontaneously, accepting the risks involved;
(d) act on their decisions, even those they fear the most;
(e) realize that few people are sufficiently actualized to nourish them;
(f) realize that all significant relationships are either deepening or deteriorating;
(g) realize that they sometimes need to 'burn bridges' in order to move forward;
(h) enjoy going their own way and having time to themselves;

(i)   experience greater joy and greater pain than other people;
(j)   can face the difficulties of functioning ahead of most others;
(k)   avoid societal traps which would restrain their potency;
(l)   accept the responsibility which comes with their skills and vision.

These characteristics are ones which professionals must strive towards if they are to develop the enabling personalities with which to empower parents of children with disabilities and their less experienced colleagues.

### 9.2.3 Habits of highly effective people

Covey (1989) has proposed that there are seven key habits which characterize highly effective people and which therefore need to be developed in order for us to become more effective in our personal and professional lives. These are briefly outlined below.

#### (a) Be proactive

Rather than waiting for things to come their way, people should decide to make small changes in the things they have influence over in order to make progress towards their goals.

#### (b) Begin with the end in mind

You should write a personal mission statement which specifies goals for each of the roles you fulfil, including all family and work roles.

#### (c) Put first things first

Prioritize all the tasks you need to complete on the basis of their urgency and importance. Use these priorities to allot time for them on a weekly plan. Within the plan it is important to keep a balance of time allotted to working or giving of yourself and that spent on 're-charging your battery'.

### (d) Think win/win

In all interactions with other people in which there is a conflict of needs it is important to find solutions which are mutually beneficial. The assertion skills, discussed in Chapter 7, are useful in this regard.

### (e) Seek to understand, then to be understood

In order to communicate most effectively it is important to use active listening skills (discussed in Chapter five) before stating your case.

### (f) Facilitate creative co-operation

Effectiveness will be increased when we initiate co-operative ventures with individuals and groups and encourage team-work among our colleagues.

### (g) Sharpen the saw

It is essential to attend to the balanced self-renewal of your capacity to give of yourself, focusing on the mental, physical, social, emotional and spiritual dimensions.

These habits are ones which professionals who seek to improve their effectiveness in working with parents and their colleagues would do well to develop. However, they are, of course, useful in increasing effectiveness in all aspects of our personal and professional lives.

## 9.3 MENTORING, EMPOWERING AND ENABLING SKILLS

Professionals who are functioning at high levels of psychological health and self-actualization and who are highly effective people themselves will be able to act as mentors for other people and work with them in ways that are empowering and enabling. The rationales for, and major components of, mentoring, empowering and enabling are discussed below.

### 9.3.1 Mentoring

Mentoring is characterized by a fairly long-term relationship between two people in which one of them supports and encourages the other person to work towards some creative achievement or to fulfil their potential in some other way. Sheehy (1981) describes a mentor as a trusted older friend who endorses the younger person's dream and helps him or her toward realizing it. A common example is that of sports coaches who take younger players 'under their wing' and do everything they can to help them develop their talents to the fullest extent. Mentoring occurs in many other situations and numerous writers have commented on its value (Covey, 1989; Levinson, 1978; Noller, 1982; Sheehy, 1974, 1981; Toffler, 1981).

Torrance (1984) suggests that the importance of mentors in facilitating creative achievement, and general success in life, has been recognized for centuries. He argues that, wherever someone is persistently creative another person has acted as a mentor, sponsor, patron or guru. This person is usually outside the creative person's peer group but has some power or influence in the field in which he or she is working. According to Torrance, mentors support and encourage mentees in expressing and testing their ideas. They also help them to develop their talents while ignoring the constraints which others attempt to impose on their creativity.

Torrance (1984) reports the results of some research which suggests that mentoring is an important and relatively frequent experience. In the study, Torrance followed up a group of 212 young adults who he had surveyed 22 years earlier when they were in primary school. He found that 40 males and 57 females had mentors. He also found that having a mentor was correlated with several indices of adult creative achievement and was a better predictor of the level of achievement of these young adults than their IQs! In addition, he found that those young adults who had mentors completed a greater number of years of education than their peers who did not have mentors. This research emphasizes the potential power of mentoring in facilitating personal development.

In fact, some of the most powerful personal experiences in my life have come about from interactions with people who have acted as mentors and others who I shall call detractors. The people who have acted as my mentors have had a tremendously enabling effect on my life by basically expressing confidence in my abilities, providing guidance when it was needed and encouraging me to strive to fulfil my ambitions. The people who have acted as detractors have had a negative impact on my life by using destructive criticism and 'put-downs', which reduced my self-confidence and slowed down my progress towards the goals I had set myself. Having experienced the effects of both mentors and detractors has convinced me of the enormous potential impact, for good or bad, of these two types of relationships on people's lives.

Professionals can make an invaluable contribution to this field by acting as mentors for some of their less experienced colleagues and also for some parents. Mentoring basically involves providing a model of a highly effective person and using enabling and empowering skills to encourage, enthuse and support people in aiming to develop their talents and fulfil their goals. Opportunities for mentoring colleagues most often occur when a professional has a supervisory relationship with a less experienced colleague, although this need not always be the case. When colleagues show an interest in working with parents more experienced professionals can act as mentors in order to help them develop their knowledge, skills and attitudes relevant to parent involvement.

Professionals can also act as mentors for parents, particularly those parents who, having come to terms with their child's disability and established stability in their family lives, feel altruistic and wish to contribute to some aspect of life outside their families. While leading training groups with parents wishing to become involved in parent-to-parent schemes (discussed in Chapter 8) my colleagues and I often become aware of parents who have a tremendous potential for contributing more extensively. By acting as mentors for these parents professionals have been able to help them use their involvement in parent-to-parent as a springboard to various other activities such as working on the committees of other voluntary organizations and setting up family support centres.

In addition to acting as mentors, professionals can also fill the important role of teaching colleagues and parents how to deal with any detractors they encounter. This can be accomplished by helping them to improve their self-esteem and by teaching them the assertion skills needed for dealing with criticism, which were discussed in Chapter 7.

### 9.3.2 Empowering

Empowering parents involves helping them to develop a sense of mastery and control over their lives. This includes helping them to identify their own resources, those available in their families, and the ones outside their families to which they would benefit from gaining access. Empowering also includes facilitating parents' problem-solving and decision-making abilities and helping them develop the behaviours required to deal effectively with people in order to obtain the resources they need (Dunst, Trivette and Deal, 1988). Empowering therefore goes beyond meeting the parents' current needs to facilitating parents' competencies and making them better able to mobilize their own resources. It therefore requires that professionals identify and develop parents' capabilities rather than allowing them to become dependent on professional help. The focus of professional interventions is therefore on facilitating the development of the knowledge, attitudes and skills which will promote the competency of all family members and strengthen overall family functioning. Deriving satisfaction from seeing parents become increasingly capable and, as soon as possible, function independently of them, is therefore an essential quality of professionals who wish to empower parents.

### 9.3.5. Enabling

Enabling involves facilitating the development of adaptive behaviours which will promote the growth of all family members. The emphasis is on personal growth rather than simply addressing current problems (Dunst, Trivette and Deal, 1988). In practice, enabling involves a range of possible strategies, the first step of which is initiated when a parent or a professional colleague seek help with a problem or concern. In this situation I first use the listening skills and counselling model, described in Chapters 5 and 6, to help the person explore their concern and work out a plan of action to deal with the situation. Counselling often ends at this point but this is where enabling begins. The first step involves supporting people in carrying out the action plans which they have chosen in order to cope with their problem situations. But enabling seeks to go beyond this in facilitating the other person's growth and fulfilment of their potential to the fullest possible extent. So people are helped to become aware of the life skill areas in which they have strengths that could be utilized and those in which they have weaknesses that need to be addressed. Enabling may therefore involve the teaching of life skills that are unrelated to the problem situations that people present with but which are in aspects of their functioning that need to be developed if they are to progress toward self-actualization (Gazda, 1984). Enabling also involves encouraging people to expand their range of options for how they will behave and building self-control and self-esteem. Finally, people are encouraged to develop their own self-help strategies such as attending growth groups, reading books on personal effectiveness (e.g. Bolton, 1979) and joining self-help groups.

Essential elements of enabling people involve helping them to live their lives more effectively, which was discussed earlier in the chapter, and helping them to adopt effective strategies for managing the stress in their lives, which is discussed below.

## 9.4 STRESS MANAGEMENT SKILLS

### 9.4.1 The need for managing stress

During my training as a psychologist, a senior colleague, who worked with children who had disabilities and their parents, gave me some sound advice about how to cope with the high stress levels which people in this field experience. He suggested that the best way to manage stress is to, 'Take a break: in the middle of the day; the middle of the week; and the middle of the year'. I have found that when I follow this piece of advice it definitely helps to reduce stress and increase my effectiveness, as well as my general enjoyment of life. As Covey (1989) has suggested (earlier in this chapter) it is important to continually recharge our batteries if our ability to give of ourselves is not to be reduced. However, the problem with advice like that from my colleague is that, even though we know that it works, we generally don't follow it. In fact, this same colleague seldom took his own advice and ended up collapsing at work and taking early retirement because of a stress-related illness!

The purpose of this section is to help professionals who work in the disability field manage stress more effectively and thereby avoid 'burning out'. It is also foreseen that these professionals will then be able to pass on stress management techniques to their colleagues and to the parents of children with disabilities with whom they work. In the first part of this section, some facts about stress and burnout are discussed and the importance of identifying the symptoms of too much stress is emphasized. Then, a comprehensive model for stress management is presented. The model includes strategies which focus on personal, interpersonal, task-related and organizational factors which need to be addressed in order to effectively manage stress.

### 9.4.2 Effects of stress

Stress can manifest itself in a wide variety of ways. When people are under severe stress it tends to first affect any areas of physical or psychological weakness which a person has. For example, the first sign that I get that stress is getting the better of me is when I begin to experience a mild form of the stammer which I had as a child. With other people the signs of too much stress may be problems with their stomach or difficulty in sleeping at night. Some people experience unusual and sometimes frightening physical symptoms such as numbness in a limb or a sensation that one has suddenly become heavier and fatter. It is important to recognize these early stress-related reactions so that lifestyle changes can be made in order to prevent burnout occurring.

The symptoms of burnout include feeling tense, exhausted or depressed. People at risk of burning out may develop negative attitudes toward other people, become generally cynical or experience little feeling of accomplishment in their personal and professional lives. They may frequently be ill, have a lot of time off work, and increase their use of drugs such as alcohol and tobacco. They are likely to also be involved in increased conflict with family and friends. Experiencing these symptoms of burnout on a long-term basis can have serious consequences for a person's psychological and physiological health. There are also substantial negative effects on organizations due to staff suffering the effects of burnout, such as excessive absenteeism, higher accident rates and health care costs, lower overall morale among staff and less effective delivery of service. Therefore, it is important, both for organizations and the personnel within them to manage stress appropriately and thereby avoid the debilitating effects of burnout. The first step in this is for everyone to recognize the early signs of burnout and to employ suitable strategies to manage the stress in their lives.

### 9.4.3 Stress management model

People are very different in the ways they cope with high levels of stress. What works for some people does not work for others. Therefore, the model for stress management, which is presented below, outlines a wide range of strategies for coping with stress from which people can choose the specific techniques most suited to themselves. However, it is important to address each of the personal, interpersonal, task related and organizational aspects of stress management in order to avoid the negative effects which stress can have on our lives. A summary of the stress management model is illustrated in Fig. 9.1. The visual representation of the model is intended to act as a reminder that the whole range of strategies should be considered when seeking to effectively manage stress.

### (a) Interpersonal responses

For most people, the majority of the stress they experience results from their relationships with other people, especially colleagues and family members (Cooper, Cooper and Eaker, 1988). For parents of children with disabilities, the professionals they must interact with in order to obtain the best services for their children can also be important sources of stress. Therefore, it is essential that both professionals and parents

**Figure 9.1** Summary of stress management model.

develop the skills of communicating assertively with other people in order to reduce the stress levels in their inter-personal relationships. Full use should be made of the asser-tion skills discussed in Chapter 7 including: saying 'no' when you need to; expressing feelings using 'I' messages; giving constructive feedback; and techniques for dealing with criticism or aggression. Working at developing mutually satisfying relationships with the significant people you have to interact with is one of the best ways of reducing stress levels.

Another strategy for reducing stress levels which is in the interpersonal domain is related to how personal concerns are dealt with. Talking over your problems with other people often helps to reduce stress. Sharing your concerns is particularly useful when the other person has experienced similar pro-blems, since this generates a feeling of 'being in the same boat' which is widely acknowledged to be therapeutic (Yalom, 1985). Having a network of colleagues, friends and family members who can provide support and a listening ear when stress levels get too high is tremendously valuable. You should therefore be continually aware of maintaining, and if possible, expanding your support network, so that in times of need there will be people available to provide support and help you cope with the stress.

Finally, when it becomes really difficult to cope with the stress you are experiencing it is important not to hold back from asking for help from other people. Many people find it very difficult to ask others for help even when they are finding it almost impossible to cope. It should be remembered that delegation is a quality of good management, that it does not make us any less worthy by asking for help and that most people enjoy helping others when they are in need. Sometimes the effects of stress are so debilitating that help from a professional counsellor would be beneficial, but this is probably the type of help which is most difficult for most people to accept. People of British descent tend to think that they must be 'dangling from the lightshade' before needing professional counselling. An example of just how helpful stress counselling can be was provided by a student of mine who was having frightening sensations of feeling heavier and fatter after experiencing two traumatic incidents within a short period of time. In a ten minute counselling session I was able to help her to get rid of these sensations by using a simple technique which involved her focusing her complete attention on these sensations (Gendlin, 1981).

### (b) Emotional responses

Useful skills for coping with stress are those which are based on centring (Laurie and Tucker, 1982), breathing (Madders, 1979) and relaxation techniques (Cautela and Groden, 1978). Hypnotism, massage and various forms of meditation involve combinations of these three types of technique and have been used for centuries to help people cope with stress. Techniques which have become popular more recently for facilitating relaxation are guided fantasy and progressive relaxation. In guided fantasy people are encouraged to close their eyes and imagine themselves in some relaxing situation such as, having a long hot bath, lying on a beach, drifting down the river on a boat, or going for a stroll in the countryside. In progressive relaxation people learn to tense and relax the various muscle groups throughout the body, from head to toe, so that they become more aware of any tension in the body and are able to relax all these muscle groups in order to achieve total relaxation. These techniques are described in detail elsewhere (Cooper, Cooper and Eaker, 1988; Hall and Hall, 1988).

Personally, although I have found both of these techniques to produce excellent levels of relaxation, I tend not to use them on a regular basis. The technique I use is much simpler and quicker and therefore fits better into my frenetic lifestyle. I use my relaxation technique whenever I feel myself tensing up or get other signs that I am under too much stress. It only takes two to three minutes and can be used when sitting, standing, lying down, driving your car, in a meeting or sitting at your desk. You simply begin to breathe in slowly through your nose and out through your mouth, breathing deeply from your stomach and not from your chest. You then run your mind quickly through your body from head to foot checking for any areas of tension. For most people tension will be located across the back of the neck or in the stomach or around the jaw and mouth. Having found where the tension is you then focus your attention on it, gently exercising the tense muscles while maintaining your attention on them and breathing deeply until the tension starts to fade. This works for me nine times out of ten, but when it isn't sufficient I use one of the more extensive techniques referred to above. While many other professionals may find this form of 'first aid' relaxation technique useful it should be borne in mind that it is clearly better to build relaxation exercises into your daily routine.

### (c) Cognitive responses

It has been shown that our emotional and physiological reactions to events are affected by the way we perceive these events (Meichenbaum, 1985). More specifically, it is the things we tell ourselves about the way we and others should act that often creates unnecessary stress. Mills (1982) points out that people tend to have unconscious rules about the way they and others ought to behave. For example:

- I must never make a mistake.
- I must do my best work at all times.
- Other people should always think highly of me.
- Other people should never disappoint me.

These unspoken rules create high levels of stress when we try to live up to them, or expect others to. Therefore, as Mills suggests, we need to make ourselves aware of our unconscious rules, challenge the thinking that accompanies them and revise them to produce less stressful messages. For example:

- I would rather not make any mistakes but if I do it just shows that I'm human.
- Although I always aim to produce my best work, sometimes this is not possible due to lack of time or energy, so it's acceptable to produce average work at these times.
- I like others to think well of me but realize that some won't and I can live with that.
- I would like everyone I have to deal with to be honest and reliable but unfortunately the world just isn't like that, so it's something I must accept.

This, of course, is much easier said than done, as an incident which occurred during some counsellor training taught me. A colleague was counselling a young woman whose main concerns were associated with her anxiety about completing a training course she was undertaking. A major problem was that her fear of making mistakes was making it difficult for her to hand in assignments. My colleague suggested that it was all right to make mistakes and that to confirm that this was the case she should make a deliberate mistake on her next assignment. She was adamant that this was something she could not do. Since I was observing the session behind a two-way mirror with a phone link to my colleague, I called him and suggested that one mistake wasn't enough; she should make several mistakes! The client was so taken aback by this that she agreed to make one mistake in the next assignment. When she next came to counselling the young woman was noticeably more relaxed and positive about herself. She recounted that she had duly made the deliberate mistake but when she got back the assignment from her tutor the mistake had not been noticed! This had led her to rethink her whole attitude to mistakes.

In addition to changing your unconscious rules it is also useful to change any negative, stress-producing thoughts to positive, calming ones (Meichenbaum, 1985; Mills, 1982). For example:

- Stay calm. You can handle this well as long as you don't lose your temper.
- Worrying about it will do no good. Whatever happens you can handle it when the time comes.
- It has been a difficult experience but there are things you have learnt from it.

By using such positive self-statements to counteract any negative thoughts you are having, your stress level can be considerably reduced.

Another way to reduce stress is through visualization (Gawain, 1982). Developing the art of positive visualization has been shown to have therapeutic effects in both personal and professional situations (Shaw, Bensky and Dixon, 1981). Visualizing yourself feeling relaxed in a situation in which you normally become tense can be helpful, as can visualizing yourself achieving a goal for which you are striving.

Finally, keeping a healthy sense of humour is a powerful strategy for managing stress. I will never forget the meeting of a group of parents who had children with heart defects which was getting more and more tense and depressing as parents talked about the various problems with their children's hearts. Several parents appeared to be getting quite upset as everyone focused on each other's tragic stories. Then at a particularly depressing moment one of the parents quipped, 'It breaks your heart doesn't it'. This was greeted with peels of laughter from everyone. The tension disappeared and the mood of the meeting lifted considerably. This incident taught me that, no matter how bleak things get, maintaining a sense of humour is a big help in managing the stress involved.

### (d) Physical responses

Taking care of yourself physically is an essential aspect of stress management. Getting adequate sleep and rest is very important.

I have noticed that when I don't get half an hour break at lunch time I am much more likely to make mistakes in the afternoon and am usually shattered by the end of the day. Having a baby in the house while writing this book has taught me that inadequate sleep on a regular basis seriously reduces my efficiency and makes me irritable.

Having a healthy diet, eating regular meals and avoiding the abuse of drugs such as alcohol, tobacco, tea and coffee are other important aspects of effective stress management (Hanson, 1987; Madders, 1979). A common response to high levels of stress is to eat more which can lead to becoming overweight. Of course, it is best not to use food for gratification when under stress but if you can't avoid doing this sometimes then it is important to make sure that you exercise regularly. Participating in vigorous exercise at least three times a week is one of the best ways to avoid the negative effects of stress. Some people like to join a gym or health club and have an organized exercise programme, others prefer regular involvement in sports such as tennis, badminton, bowling or golf. However, the best exercises for the body as a whole are thought to be swimming and brisk walking. Ideally, exercise should be built into your daily routine, for example, by walking to work or having a lunchtime jog every day.

Another important aspect of stress management is the need for a change of environment from time to time. Mills (1982) suggests getting completely away from home and work environments on vacation at least once a year and also taking some weekends off to 'get away from it all'. It's also important to have changes of scene built into your weekly routine. I find that in playing sports such as golf and badminton I meet up with people from a wide range of occupations which is quite refreshing. Other people fulfil this same function through hobbies or clubs they are involved in. Often when people become very busy with work or family commitments it is these kind of activities which end up being cut out. This applies to professionals as well as parents of children with disabilities and it increases the risk of 'burning-out'.

When people consider that they cannot justify taking the time needed for a regular sporting, hobby or club involvement it is important for them to realize that a few minutes a day devoted to what my colleague Ray Murray calls 'nurturing themselves', can achieve a similar end. The concept of 'nurturing yourself' is something that I now include in all my work with groups of parents. I find that most parents are so heavily involved in caring for their children with disabilities that they tend not to think about their own needs, which puts them at greater risk of experiencing the negative effects of stress. Typically, parents (particularly mothers) are quite shocked when they are asked to spend ten to fifteen minutes during the next week doing something that is just for themselves; something which they really want to do, not which they think they ought to do. Activities chosen range from having a long soak in the bath to phoning a friend for a chat. Feedback from parents on this task suggests that it is a revelation to many of them to take time to nurture themselves, but having tried it out they have felt so much happier that they decide to make it a regular feature of their lives.

I consider that getting the right balance of work and play is probably the key to managing stress effectively. During the final stages of writing this book I had a month in Barbados where I worked on the book for most of the day, then had a swim in the sea and spent time with my family in the evening. My productivity on the book and enjoyment of life was greater in these four weeks than at any time of the writing period. Oh, how I wish I could maintain this balance all the year round!

### (e) Task-related responses

A key component of coping with stress for busy people is managing time as efficiently as possible. Much has been written about this topic in recent years (Black, 1987; Ferner, 1980; Fontana, 1993; Turla and Hawkins, 1985). According to this literature the essential elements of time management are establishing priorities and carefully planning the use of your time. Covey (1989) has produced a useful weekly worksheet for doing just this. He suggests that we first of all analyse the various roles which we fill such as husband, son, father, lecturer, clinician, researcher, colleague, friend, neighbour, team-mate. Next we should consider what goals we have in each of these areas and work out our priorities for these for the following week. Then we need to allot time on the worksheet (or in our diaries) to work on our prioritized goals over the next week.

Other important aspects of time management include: delegating as many tasks as you possibly can; saying 'no' to new responsibilities you don't want to take on; and making daily lists of jobs to be done. One strategy I have found particularly useful is forcing myself to handle each thing which comes to me on paper only once, if at all possible. Most letters and memos I deal with on the spot, whether this means writing a note back to the person on the bottom of their memo or perusing a document and filing it in the circular file! Only things which can't be dealt with immediately are put on my desk for later attention. Another important strategy is not to waste time in meetings. The meetings I organize are kept short and to the point. In most cases I allot a maximum of an hour to the meetings which are essential for me to attend and walk out when the hour is up. My rationale for this is that an efficiently run meeting should be over in an hour with any items needing longer consideration being delegated to an individual or sub-committee to look into and report back to the next meeting.

Another important aspect of time management for me is ensuring that the most intellectually demanding tasks are done at the time of day when I'm at my best. Thus, I tend to write early in the day and leave other less demanding tasks until later. Also, I find that 'Grandma's Rule' usually works for me. That is, I promise myself a break or a snack after each hour of work and force myself to go at least an hour before I get my reward!

A common problem is that people often procrastinate on tasks because they seem so overwhelming when all that needs to be done is considered. In this situation it is generally useful to do a simple 'task analysis', that is, break the task down into manageable components and tackle it step by step. Focusing on one step at a time helps prevent being overwhelmed by the enormity of the task.

Another strategy which is quite useful in dealing with pro-crastination I have called 'Garry's Rule'. It is based on the observation that when there is an unpleasant task to do people tend to put it off until another task, even more unpleasant, has to be done. When this occurs the first task begins to appear attractive. For example, one of my least favourite jobs is marking assignments so this tends not to get done until it becomes necessary to do something like mow the lawn or vacuum the floors. Although I don't enjoy either of these jobs and always put them off as long as I can, they appear quite attractive in comparison with doing my marking, so tend to be tackled instead of the marking. However, the interesting thing about this situation is that after ten minutes of vacuuming, marking the assignments becomes quite attractive!

### (f) Organizational responses

Much of the stress which professionals experience is caused by organizational factors at their place of work, such as poor communication between administrators and staff or an incompetent head of department. Of course, the most effective long-term strategy to deal with such difficulties can be to bring about constructive change by becoming as involved as possible in the management of your workplace. However, such organizational factors are often ones which individuals can do little to change without expending enormous amounts of energy, so instead, it is frequently best to adopt specific strategies to manage these work-related stressors.

One way of reducing stress at work is to develop collaborative working relationships with colleagues who are open to this. As Covey (1989) suggests, initiating co-operative ventures with individuals or small groups of colleagues encourages teamwork and tends to increase everyone's effectiveness. Additionally, it is sometimes possible to get together a small group of colleagues into a support group. This can be a fairly formal group which could perhaps meet at lunch times, or it can be quite informal with a few people getting together over a drink once a week. Either way, this can be very supportive and is a useful strategy for reducing stress levels.

Another useful strategy is to keep a clear distinction between work and home by leaving all incomplete work on your office desk rather than bringing it home. It is usually better, if something has to be finished, to stay a little longer at work to get it done rather than bringing it home and having it ruin your evening or weekend. The time in my life when I have had the lowest level of work-related stress was when I had a nine-to-five job as a psychologist. Nearly all my other jobs have involved some preparation and marking done outside work hours, and it is this which I find creates most of my stress.

An important strategy to control work-related stress is not to lose sight of your career aspirations. Seeing your job as a step on the way to where you want to be in a few years' time is a way of keeping current problems in perspective. Losoncy (1982) suggests that we should continually attend to self-promotion activities. That is, we should always allocate some of our work time to develop something that will help us move towards our career goals.

Finally, a last resort strategy, to use when stress at work has become so severe that you are struggling to cope, is to take a 'mental health day' (Shaw, Bensky and Dixon, 1981). It is clearly better to take one day off and re-charge your batteries than to wait until your physical or psychological health breaks down, at which time you could need to take much longer off. Mental health days also act as a reminder that no-one is indispensable. Actually, I like to remind people who think they have to carry on because they are indispensable that, 'Death is nature's way of telling you to slow down'.

## 9.5 SUMMARY

The importance of professionals in the field of childhood disability being enabling individuals who facilitate the development of parents as people rather than simply helping them to overcome their difficulties is the focus of this chapter. The basic elements of psychological health and personal effectiveness are described and the value of enabling, empowering and mentoring skills is discussed. It is proposed that professionals need stress management skills in order to cope with the high levels of stress involved in working in this field and also so that they can teach parents and their colleagues the skills necessary to reduce the stress which they experience. A stress management model is presented which suggests coping strategies that focus on interpersonal, emotional, cognitive, physical, organizational, and task-related responses to stress.

# 10

# Epilogue

The main argument of this book has been that professionals who work with children or adults with disabilities increase their effectiveness by developing collaborative working relationships with parents. Also that, if families which include individuals with disabilities are to function well and provide optimum care for all of their members, then professionals must address the needs of the family as a whole. In addition, there is a growing realization that many parents are willing and able to contribute, not only to the habilitation of their own children, but also to the field of disability on a broader scale.

However, training programmes for professionals who work with people with disabilities in the health education and social welfare fields typically include little or nothing on the skills, attitudes and knowledge necessary for effective collaboration with parents. In addition, training courses for professional counsellors generally pay little attention to working with people with disabilities and their families and few practising counsellors have expertise in this area. Even if specialist counsellors were widely available it is doubtful whether parents, in countries such as Great Britain and India, would be prepared to seek counselling because of the stigma involved and lack of understanding about its value. Whereas, parents will take their concerns to professionals who work directly with their children, such as physiotherapists, doctors, health visitors, teachers, social workers and psychologists. Therefore, since they are likely to be the main source of guidance and counselling for families who have members with disabilities, it is left to practitioners like these to do their best to develop the necessary skills.

In attempting to help in this task, this book has focused on the interpersonal skills, attitudes and knowledge which professionals require in order to work effectively with parents of children and adults with disabilities. Models for the adaptation process and for family functioning have been considered, along with a discussion of the effects on individual members of such families. The personal accounts of two parents of children with different disabilities have provided support for issues raised by the theory and research which has been presented. A theoretical model for working with parents has been proposed which suggests guidelines for practice and specifies the interpersonal skills which professionals need to develop in order to work effectively with parents. The techniques involved in listening, counselling, assertion, enabling and group work with parents are regarded as essential in this endeavour and have been discussed in detail in order to help professionals to develop their skills in these areas.

Training professionals in the interpersonal skills, attitudes and knowledge necessary for working effectively with parents need not be lengthy. The author has developed a 30-hour training course which includes the knowledge and attitudes regarding parent involvement contained in this book, plus basic training in listening and counselling skills (Hornby, 1990; Hornby and Peshawaria, 1991). More advanced training programmes, which have focused on assertion skills and group work skills, have been taught to groups of professionals in courses of from 10 to 20 hours in length.

This book is intended to contribute to the training of professionals in the competencies required for working with parents and other family members of individuals with disabilities. The book has been written so that it can be read separately or be used in conjunction with training in interpersonal skills, which of course would be the ideal situation. Either way, it is hoped that the book will help professionals to improve their practice in working with families who have members with disabilities.

# References

Allan, J.A.B. and Nairne, J.(1984) *Class Discussions for Teachers and Counsellors in the Elementary School*, University of Toronto Press, Toronto.

Allen, D.A. and Affleck, G. (1985) Are we stereotyping parents? A postscript to Blacher. *Mental Retardation*, **23** (4), 200-2.

Attwood, T. (1978) The Croydon workshop for parents of preschool mentally handicapped children. *Child: Care, Health and Development*, **4**, 79-97.

Attwood, T. (1979) The Croydon workshop for parents of severely handicapped school-age children. *Child: Care, Health and Development*, **5**, 177-88.

Batshaw, M.L., Perret, Y.M. and Carter, W.P. (1992) *Children with Disabilities: A Medical Primer*, 3rd edn, Paul H. Brookes, Baltimore.

Beck, A.T. (1976) *Cognitive Therapy and Emotional Disorders*, International Universities Press, New York.

Bell, R.Q. (1968) A reinterpretation of the direction of effects in studies of socialization. *Psychological Review*, **75** (2), 81-95.

Berger, N. (1984) Social network interventions for families that have a handicapped child, in *Families with Handicapped Members* (ed. J.C. Hansen), Aspen, Rockvill, MD, pp. 127-37.

Berger, M. and Foster, M. (1986) Applications of family therapy theory to research and interventions with families with mentally retarded children, in *Families of Handicapped Persons: Research, Programs and Policy Issues*, (eds J.J. Gallagher and P.M. Vietze) Paul H. Brookes, Baltimore, pp. 251-60.

Bicknell, J. (1988) The psychopathology of handicap, in *Living with Mental Handicap: Transitions in the Lives of People with Mental Handicaps*, (eds G. Horobin and D. May), Jessica Kingsley, London, pp. 22-37.

Blacher, J. (1984) Sequential stages of parental adjustment to the birth of a child with handicaps: Fact or artifact? *Mental Retardation*, **22** (2), 55-68.

Black, R. (1987) *Getting Things Done*, Michael Joseph, London.

Bleck, E.E. and Nagle, D.A. (1975) *Physically Handicapped Children:*

*A Medical Atlas for Teachers*, Grune & Stratton, New York.

Bolton, R. (1979) *People Skills*, Prentice-Hall, Englewood Cliffs, NJ.

Bower, S.A. and Bower, G.H. (1976) *Asserting Yourself*, Addison-Wesley, Reading,MA.

Bowlby, J. (1965) *Child Care and the Growth of Love*, 2nd edn, Penguin, Harmondsworth.

Brammer, L.M. (1988) *The Helping Relationship*, 4th edn, Prentice-Hall, Englewood Cliffs, NJ.

Bristol, M.M. and Gallagher, J.J. (1986) Research on fathers of young handicapped children, in *Families of Handicapped Persons: Research, Program and Policy Issues* (eds J.J. Gallagher & P.M. Vietze), Paul H. Brookes, Baltimore, pp. 81–100.

Bronfenbrenner, U. (1977) Towards an experimental ecology of human development. *American Psychologist*, **32** (7), 513–31.

Bronfenbrenner, U. (1979) *The Ecology of Human Development*, Harvard University Press, Cambridge, MA.

Brotherson, M.J., Turnbull, A.P., Summers, J.A. and Turnbull, H.R. (1986) Fathers of disabled children, in *The Developing Father*, (eds B.E. Robinson and R.L. Barrett) Guilford, New York, pp. 193–217.

Browning, E. (1987) *I Can't See What You're Saying*, Angel Press, Chichester.

Carkhuff, R. and Berenson, B. (1967) *Beyond Counselling and Therapy*, Holt, Rinehart & Winston, Toronto.

Carter, E. and McGoldrick, M. (eds) (1980) *The Family Life Cycle: A Framework for Family Therapy*, Gardner, New York.

Cautela, J.R. and Groden, J. (1978) *Relaxation*, Research Press, Champaign, Ill.

Chilman, C.S., Nunnally, E.W. and Cox, F.M. (eds) (1988) *Chronic Illness and Disability*, Sage, Newbury Park, CA.

Chinn, P.C., Winn, J. and Walters, R.H. (1978) *Two Way Talking with Parents of Special Children*, C.V. Mosby, St. Louis.

Cole, D.R. (1982) *Helping*, Butterworths, Toronto.

Cooper, C.L., Cooper, R.D. and Eaker, L.H. (1988) *Living with Stress*, Penguin, London.

Coopersmith, E.I. (ed.) (1984) *Family Therapy with Families with Handicapped Children*, Aspen, Rockville, MD.

Cotler, S.B. and Guerra, J.J. (1976) *Assertion Training*, Research Press, Champaign, Ill.

Covey, S.R. (1989) *Seven Habits of Highly Effective People*, Simon & Shuster, New York.

Crnic, K.A. and Leconte, J.M. (1986) Understanding sibling needs and influences, in *Families with Handicapped Children*, (eds R. Fewell and P.F. Vadasy) PRO-ED, Austin, TX, 75–98.

Cunningham, C.C. and Jeffree, D.M. (1975) The organization and structure of workshops for parents of mentally handicapped children. *Bulletin of the British Psychological Society*, **28**, 405–11.

Cunningham, C.C., Morgan, P.H. and McGucken, R.B. (1984) Down's syndrome: Is dissatisfaction with disclosure of diagnosis inevitable? *Developmental Medicine and Child Neurology*, **26**, 33–39.

Dinkmeyer, D.C. and Muro, J.J. (1979) *Group Counselling: Theory and Practice*, 2nd edn, Peacock, Itasca, III.

Dunst, C.J., Trivette, C.M. and Deal, A.G. (1988) *Enabling and Empowering Families: Principles and Guidelines for Practice*, Brookline Books, Cambridge, MA.

Egan, G. (1982) *The Skilled Helper*, 2nd edn, Brooks/Cole, Monterey, CA.

Egan, G. (1984) Skilled helping: A problem management framework for helping and helper training, in *Teaching Psychological Skills*, (ed. D. Larson) Brooks/Cole, Monterey, CA, pp. 133–50.

Egan, G. (1990) *The Skilled Helper*, 4th edn, Brooks/Cole, Monterey, CA.

Ellis, A. (1974) *Disputing Irrational Beliefs*, Institute for Rational Living, New York.

Featherstone, H. (1981) *A Difference in the Family*, Penguin, Harmondsworth.

Ferner, J.D. (1980) *Successful Time Management*, Wiley, New York.

Ferrari, M. (1984) Chronic illness: psychosocial effects on siblings – 1. Chronically ill boys. *Journal of Child Psychology and Psychiatry*, **25**, 459–76.

Fewell, R.R. and Vadasy, P.F. (eds) (1986) *Families of Handicapped Children*, Pro-Ed, Austin, TX.

Fontana, D. (1993) *Managing Time*, British Psychological Society, Leicester.

Forehand, R., Wells, K.C. and Griest, D.L. (1980) An examination of the social validity of a parent training program. *Behavior Therapy*, **11**, 488–502.

Foster, M. and Berger, M. (1985) Research with families with handicapped children: A multilevel systemic perspective, in *The Handbook of Family Psychology and Therapy* (ed. L. L'Abate), Dorsey, Homewood, Ill, pp.741–80.

Frankl, V. (1965) *The Doctor and the Soul, from Psychotherapy to Logotherapy*, 2nd edn, Knopf, New York.

Fullwood, D. and Cronin, P. (1986) *Facing the Crowd: Managing Other People's Insensitivities to Your Disabled Child*, Royal Victorian Institute for the Blind, Melbourne.

Furneaux, B. (1988) *Special Parents*, Open University Press, Milton Keynes.

Gallagher, J.J. Beckman, P. and Cross, A.H. (1983) Families of handicapped children: Sources of stress and its amelioration. *Exceptional Children*, **50**, 10–19.

Gallagher, J.J., Scharfman, W. and Bristol, M.M. (1984) The division of responsibilities in families with preschool handicapped and non-handicapped children. *Journal for the Division of Early Childhood*, **8**, 3–11.

Gargiulo, R.M. (1985) *Working with Parents of Exceptional Children: A Guide for Professionals*, Houghton Mifflin, Boston.

Gath, A. (1977) The impact of an abnormal child upon the parents. *British*

*Journal of Psychiatry*, **130**, 405–10.

Gath, A. and Gumley, D. (1984) Down's syndrome and the family: follow-up of children first seen in infancy. *Developmental Medicine & Child Neurology*, **26**, 500–508.

Gawain, S. (1982) *Creative Visualization*, Bantam, New York.

Gazda, G.M. (1984) Multiple impact training: A life skills approach, in *Teaching Psychological Skills*, (ed. D. Larson) Brooks/Cole, Monterey, CA, pp. 89–103.

Gendlin, E.T. (1981) *Focusing*, Bantam, New York.

George, J.D. (1988) Therapeutic intervention for grandparents and extended family of children with developmental delays. *Mental Retardation*, **26** (6), 369–75.

Gitterman, A. and Shulman, L. (eds) (1986) *Mutual Aid Groups and the Life Cycle*, Peacock, Itasca, Ill.

Gordon, T. (1970) *Parent Effectiveness Training*, Wyden, New York.

Grossman, F. (1972) *Brothers and Sisters of Retarded Children*, Syracuse University Press, Syracuse, NY.

Hall, E. and Hall, C. (1988) *Human Relations in Education*, Routledge, London.

Hannam, C. (1988) *Parents and Mentally Handicapped Children*, 3rd edn, Bristol Classical Press, Bristol.

Hanson, P. (1987) *The Joy of Stress*, Pan, London.

Hatch, S. and Hinton, T. (1986) *Self-Help in Practice*, Joint Unit for Social Services Research, Sheffield.

Havinghurst, R.J. (1972) *Developmental Tasks and Education*, 3rd edn, David McKay, New York.

Hebden, J. (1985) *She'll Never Do Anything, Dear*, Souvenir Press, London.

Holland, S. and Ward, C. (1990) *Assertiveness: A Practical Approach*, Winslow Press, Bicester.

Hornby, G. (1982) Meeting the counselling and guidance needs of parents with intellectually handicapped children. *Mental Handicap in New Zealand*, **6**, 8–27.

Hornby, G. (1987) Families with exceptional children, in *Exceptional Children in New Zealand*, (eds D.R. Mitchell and N.N. Singh) Dunmore Press, Palmerston North, NZ, pp. 118–29.

Hornby, G. (1988) Launching Parent to Parent Schemes. *British Journal of Special Education*, **15** (2), 77–78.

Hornby, G. (1989) A model for parent participation. *British Journal of Special Education*, **16** (4), 161–62.

Hornby, G. (1990) Training teachers to work with parents of children with special educational needs. *British Journal of In-Service Education*, **16** (2), 116–18.

Hornby, G. (1991) Parent involvement, in *Early Intervention Studies for Young Children with Special Needs* (eds D. Mitchell and R.I. Brown) Chapman & Hall, London. pp. 206–25.

Hornby, G. (1992a) A review of fathers' accounts of their experiences of parenting children with disabilities. *Disability, Handicap and Society,* **7** (4), 363–74.

Hornby, G. (1992b) Group parent training using reflective counselling and behavioural training procedures. *British Journal of Mental Subnormality,* **38** (2), 79–86.

Hornby, G. (1993) Effects of children with Down syndrome on families: Fathers' views. *Journal of Child and Family Studies,* in press.

Hornby, G. (1994) Effects on fathers of children with Down syndrome. *Journal of Child and Family Studies,* in press.

Hornby, G. and Ashworth, T. (1994) Grandparent support for families who have children with disabilities: A survey of parents. *Journal of Child and Family Studies,* in press.

Hornby, G. and Murray, R. (1983) Group programmes for parents of children with various handicaps. *Child: Care, Health and Development,* **9**, 185–98.

Hornby, G., Murray, R. and Davies, L. (1993) *Parent to Parent: Basic Helping/Supporting Skills: Leader's Manual,* Auckland College of Education, Auckland, NZ.

Hornby, G., Murray, R. and Jones, R. (1987) Establishing a Parent to Parent service. *Child: Care, Health and Development,* **13**, 277–88.

Hornby, G. and Peshawaria, R.P. (1991) Teaching counselling skills for working with parents of mentally handicapped children in a developing country. *International Journal of Special Education,* **6** (2), 231–36.

Hornby, G. and Seligman, M. (1991) Disability and the family: Current status and future developments. *Counselling Psychology Quarterly,* **4** (4), 267–71.

Hornby, G. and Singh, N.N. (1982) Reflective group counselling for parents of mentally retarded children. *British Journal of Mental Subnormality,* **28**, 71–76.

Hornby, G. and Singh, N.N. (1983) Group training for parents of mentally retarded children. A review and methodological analysis. *Child: Care, Health and Development,* **9** (3), 199–213.

Hornby, G. and Singh, N.N. (1984) Behavioural group training with parents of mentally retarded children. *Journal of Mental Deficiency Research,* **28**, 43–52.

Jakubowski, P. and Lange, A.J. (1978) *The Assertive Option,* Research Press, Champaign, Ill.

Knight, B. (1978) *Your Feelings are Your Friends,* Hodder & Stoughton, Auckland, NZ.

Kroth, R.L. (1985) *Communicating with Parents of Exceptional Children,* 2nd edn, Love, Denver.

Kubler-Ross, E. (1969) *On Death and Dying,* Macmillan, New York.

Lamb, M.E. (1983) Fathers of exceptional children, in *The Family with a Handicapped Child,* (ed. M. Seligman) Grune & Stratton, New York, pp. 125–46.

Lansdown, R. (1980) *More than Sympathy: The Everyday Needs of Sick and Handicapped Children and their Families,* Tavistock, London.

Laurie, S.G. and Tucker, M.J. (1982) *Centering*, Excalibur, Wellingborough.

Lehr, S. and Lehr, R. (1990) Getting what you want: Expectations of families, in *Quality Assurance for Individuals with Developmental Disabilities* (eds V.J. Bradley and H.A. Bersani) Paul H. Brookes, Baltimore, pp. 61–75.

Levinson, D.J. (1978) *The Seasons of a Man's Life*, Ballantine, New York.

Lombana, J.H. (1989) Counselling persons with disabilities: Summary and predictions. *Journal of Counselling and Development*, **68**, 177–79.

Lonsdale, G. (1978) Family life with a handicapped child: The parents speak. *Child: Care, Health and development*, **4**, 99–120.

Losoncy, L. (1982) *Think Your Way To Success*, Wiltshire, Hollywood, CA.

Madders, J. (1979) *Stress and Relaxation*, Collins, Sydney.

Manthei, M. (1981) *Positively Me: A Guide to Assertive Behaviour*, (revised edn), Methuen, Auckland, NZ.

Marshak, L.E. and Seligman, M.(1993) *Counselling Persons with Physical Disabilities*, PRO-ED, Austin, TX.

Maslow, A. (1962) *Toward a Psychology of Being*, Van Nostrand, New York.

Max, L. (1985) Parents' views of provisions, services and research, in *Mental Retardation in New Zealand*, (eds N.N. Singh and K.M. Wilton) Whitcoulls, Christchurch, pp. 250–62.

McAndrew, I. (1976) Children with a handicap and their families. *Child: Care, Health and Development*, **2**, 213–37.

McConachie, H. (1986) *Parents and Young Mentally Handicapped Children: A Review of Research Issues*, Croom Helm, London.

McConkey, R. (1985) *Working with Parents: A Practical Guide for Teachers and Therapists*, Croom Helm, London.

McConkey, R. and McCormack, C. (1983) *Breaking Barriers*, Souvenir Press, London.

Meichenbaum, D (1985) *Stress Inoculation Training*, Pergamon, New York.

Meyer, D.J. (1986a) Fathers of handicapped children, in *Families of Handicapped Children* (eds R.R. Fewell and P.F. Vadasy) PRO-ED, Austin, TX, pp. 35–73.

Meyer, D.J. (1986b) Fathers of children with mental handicaps, in *The Father's Role: Applied Perspectives* (ed. M.E. Lamb) Wiley, New York, pp. 227–54.

Meyer, D.J., Vadasy, P.F. and Fewell, R.R. (1985) *Sibshops; A Handbook for Implementing Workshops for Siblings of Children with Special Needs*, University of Washington Press, Seattle.

Meyer, D.J., Vadasy, P.F., Fewell, R.R. and Schell, G.C. (1985) *A Handbook for the Fathers Program*, University of Washington Press, Seattle.

Mills, J.W. (1982) *Coping with Stress*, Wiley, New York.

Mink, I.T. and Nihira, K. (1987) Direction of effects: Family life styles and behaviour of TMR children. *American Journal of Mental Deficiency*, **92** (1), 57–64.

Minnes, P.M. (1988) Family stress associated with a developmentally handicapped child, in *International Review of Research in Mental Retardation* (ed. N.W. Bray) vol. 15, Academic Press, London, pp. 195–226.

Mitchell, D.R. (1985) Guidance needs and counselling of parents of persons with intellectual handicaps, in *Mental Retardation in New Zealand* (eds. N.N. Singh and K.M. Wilton) Whitcoulls, Christchurch, NZ, pp. 136–56.

Murphy, M.A. (1982) The family with a handicapped child: A review of the literature. *Developmental and Behavioral Pediatrics*, **3**, 73–82.

Noller, R.B. (1982) *Mentoring: A voiced scarf*, Bearly, New York.

Olshansky, S. (1962) Chronic sorrow: A response to having a mentally defective child. *Social Casework*, **43**, 190–93.

Parke, R.D. (1986) Fathers, families and support systems, in *Families of Handicapped Persons: Research, Programs and Policy Issues*, (eds J.J. Gallagher and P.M. Vietze) Paul H. Brookes, Baltimore, pp. 101–13.

Philip, M. and Duckworth, D.(1982) *Children with Disabilities and their Families: A Review of the Research*, NFER-Nelson, Windsor.

Pieper, E. (1976) Grandparents can help. *The Exceptional Parent*, April, 7–9.

Roesel, R. and Lawlis, G.F. (1983) Divorce in families of genetically handicapped/mentally retarded individuals. *American Journal of Family Therapy*, **11** (1), 45–50.

Rogers, C.R. (1980) *A Way of Being*, Houghton Mifflin, Boston.

Roos, P. (1963) Psychological counselling with parents of retarded children. *Mental Retardation*, **1**, 345–50.

Roos, P. (1978) Parents of mentally retarded children: Misunderstood and mistreated, in *Parents Speak Out*, (eds H.R. Turnbull and A.P. Turnbull) Charles E. Merrill, Columbus, OH, pp. 245–57.

Rose, S.D. (1977) *Group Therapy: A Behavioural Approach*, Prentice-Hall, Englewood Cliffs, NJ.

Ross, A.O. (1964) *The Exceptional Child in the Family*, Grune & Stratton, New York.

Schilling, R.F. (1988) Helping families with developmentally disabled members, in *Chronic Illness and Disability*, (eds C.S. Chilman, E.W. Nunnally and F.M. Cox) Sage, Newbury Park, CA, pp. 171–92.

Seligman, M. (1979) *Strategies for Helping Parents of Exceptional Children: A Guide for Teachers*, Free Press, New York.

Seligman, M. (ed.) (1991) *The Family with a Handicapped Child*, 2nd edn, Allyn and Bacon, Boston.

Seligman, M. and Darling, R.B. (1989) *Ordinary Families: Special Children*, Guilford, New York.

Shaw, S.F., Bensky, J.M. and Dixon, B. (1981) *Stress and Burnout*, Council for Exceptional Children, Reston, VA.

Sheehy, G. (1974) *Passages: Predictable Crises in Adult Life*, E.P. Dutton, New York.

Sheehy, G. (1981) *Pathfinders*, William Morrow, New York.

Simeonsson, R.J. and McHale, S. (1981): Review: Research on handicapped children: Sibling relationships. *Child: Care, Health and Development*, **7**, 153–71.

Simpson, R.L. (1990) *Conferencing Parents of Exceptional Children*, 2nd edn, PRO-ED, Austin, TX.

Sonnek, I.M. (1986) Grandparents and the extended family of handicapped children, in *Families of Handicapped Children*, (eds R.R. Fewell and P.F. Vadasy) PRO-ED, Austin, TX, pp. 99–120.

Stewart, J.C. (1986) *Counselling Parents of Exceptional Children*, 2nd edn, Merrill, Columbus, OH.

Stone, J. and Taylor, F. (1977) *A Handbook for Parents with a Handicapped Child*, Arrow, London.

Sue, D.W., Arredondo, P. and McDavis, R.J. (1992) Multicultural counselling competencies and standards: A call to the profession. *Journal of Counselling and Development*, **70**, 477–86.

Tavormina, J.B. (1975) Relative effectiveness of behavioral and reflective group counselling with parents of mentally retarded children. *Journal of Consulting and Clinical Psychology*, **43**, 22–31.

Tavormina, J.B, Hampson, R.B. and Luscomb, R. (1976) Participant evaluations of the effectiveness of their parent counselling groups. *Mental Retardation*, **14**, 8–9.

Telford, C.W. and Sawrey, J.M. (1981) *The Exceptional Individual*, Prentice Hall, Englewood Cliffs, NJ.

Tew, B.J., Payne, E.H. and Lawrence, K.M. (1974) Must a family with a handicapped child be a handicapped family? *Developmental Medicine and Child Neurology*, **16**, 95–98.

Thompson, L. (1986) *Bringing Up a Mentally Handicapped Child*, Thorsons, Wellingborough.

Toffler, A. (1981) *The Third Wave*, Bantam, New York.

Torrance, E.P. (1984) *Mentor Relationships*, Bearly, Buffalo, NY.

Turla, P. and Hawkins, K.L. (1985) *Time Management Made Easy*, Grafton, London.

Turnbull, A.P. and Turnbull, H.R. (1986) *Families, Professionals and Exceptionality*, Merrill, Columbus, OH.

Turnbull, A.P., Summers, J.A. and Brotherson, M.J. (1984) *Working with Families with Disabled Members*, University of Kansas Press, Kansas.

Vadasy, P.F., Fewell, R.R. and Meyer, D.J. (1986) Grandparents of children with special needs: Insights into their experiences and concerns. *Journal of the Division for Early Childhood*, **10** (1), 36–44.

Webster, E.J. and Ward, L.M. (1993) *Working with Parents of Young Children with Disabilities*, Singular, San Diego, CA.

Wikler, L. (1981) Chronic stresses in families of mentally retarded children. *Family Relations*, **30**, 281–88.

Wikler, L. (1986) Periodic stresses of families of older mentally retarded children: An exploratory study. *American Journal of Mental Deficiency*, **90**, 703–6.

Wikler, L., Wasow, M. and Hatfield, E. (1981) Chronic sorrow revisited. *American Journal of Orthopsychiatry*, **51**, 63–70.

Worden, J.W. (1983) *Grief Counselling and Grief Therapy*, Tavistock, London.

Wright, J.S., Granger, R.D. and Sameroff, A.J. (1984) Parental acceptance and developmental handicap, in *Severely Handicapped Young Children and their Families*, (ed. J. Blacher) Academic Press, Orlando, pp. 51–90.

Yalom, I.D. (1985) *The Theory and Practice of Group Psychotherapy*, 3rd edn, Basic Books, New York.

# Author index

# Subject index